# Barabbas
## Son of a Father

Basil B. Clark

WALDENHOUSE PUBLISHERS, INC.
WALDEN, TENNESSEE

Barabbas, Son of a Father

Copyright © 2015 Basil B. Clark. All rights reserved.

Any unauthorized reprint or use of this material is prohibited. No part of this book whether art or text may be reproduced or transmitted in any form or by any means, electronic or mechanical, including photocopying, recording, or by any information storage and retrieval system without express written permission from the author except in the case of brief quotations embodied in critical articles and reviews.

All scripture quotations, unless otherwise indicated, are taken from the Holy Bible, New International Version®, NIV®. Copyright ©1973, 1978, 1984, 2011 by Biblica, Inc. Used by permission of Zondervan. All rights reserved worldwide. www.zondervan.com. The "NIV" and "New International Version" are trademarks registered in the United States Patent and Trademark Office by Biblica, Inc.™

ISBN: 978-1-935186-64-9

Library of Congress Control Number: 2015919236

A fictional account of Barabbas, a lesser known Biblical character. All that is known about him is that he was an insurrectionist condemned by the Romans to die, until his path intersected with that of Jesus Christ. Barabbas was set free as Jesus was crucified in his place. -- Provided by Publisher

Published by Waldenhouse Publishers, Inc.
100 Clegg Street, Signal Mountain, Tennessee 37377 USA
www.waldenhouse.com   888-222-8228
Printed in the United States of America

# ENDORSEMENTS

Barabbas who? Basil Clark, in his unique style, has reached deep into the Bible archives of the lesser known and brought to us a warm, heart changing story of a man whose life was filled with pain and anguish. This story will force each of us to search our hearts and remember the challenge that we each faced as we came to grips in our relationship with Jesus.

In Clark's writings, Barabbas takes on flesh and blood, not just a name, being revealed as a person with a dark side, yet one who was drawn into fascination with Jesus. Even though his encounter with Jesus was not spiritually motivated, one cannot hang around such a Person as Jesus without feeling the effects of such a friendship.

BARABBAS is well written and will keep your interest from start to finish, causing one to realize what life would have been like during the days of Jesus in and around Jerusalem.

*Aaron C. Reaves, Clinical Chaplain, Walker State Prison, Rock Spring, GA*

. . . . . . . . . . . . . . . . . . . . . . . . . . . . . . . . . . . . . . . . . . . . . . . . . . . . . . . . . . . . . . . . . . . . .

Basil Clark, by way of BARABBAS, once again reminds us that we are never separated from the presence of God. And again we see that putting priority on our family unit is also a main concern of our Heavenly Father.

*Nellie Cunningham, Riva, Maryland*

. . . . . . . . . . . . . . . . . . . . . . . . . . . . . . . . . . . . . . . . . . . . . . . . . . . . . . . . . . . . . . . . . . . . .

I started reading BARABBAS, became pulled into the story, and was unable to put it down until completion. How Barabbas interacted with Jesus in a way that changed his heart and life spoke to me, as I think it will to you.

*Mildred Smith, Robbinsville, North Carolina*

. . . . . . . . . . . . . . . . . . . . . . . . . . . . . . . . . . . . . . . . . . . . . . . . . . . . . . . . . . . . . . . . . . . . .

Basil Clark made the almost unknown character, Barabbas of the Bible, become a real person that I could relate to. I found myself immersed in all the characters of this story. I believe I now have some insight into what it would have been like to live during the time of Jesus.

*Carmen Koster Rhine, Corrections Officer, Nelsonville, Ohio*

Unlike the shadowy Barabbas of the gospels, Clark's Barabbas takes on flesh and blood and the passion of a revolutionary and the guilt and anguish of a driven man. Pushed into relief by conflict, both personal and political, the man appears, but then, not just a man, but everyman who ever asked, "Why was I of all people in history, the one whose life intersected with Jesus at this critical time?" This Barabbas, as ambitious revolutionary and neglectful husband and father, becomes a credible personal witness and reasonable inter-preter of the events of the last days of Jesus in a way that posits plausible answers to some of history's most enigmatic mysteries, while at the same time, drags the conversation forward into the Twenty-First Century.

*Sydney England, Associate Professor of English, University of Pikeville*

Basil Clark has done it again! Through BARABBAS, he has given us a window into the mind and motivations of a man who scripture has named, history has remembered, and people of faith have often times forgotten. This book will challenge you to hear your own voice through a character that scripture has left silent. Listen to this voice and be surprised by its insights.

*Rev. Rob Musick, University Chaplain, University of Pikeville, Kentucky*

BARABBAS has all the elements of a good story. The characters are interesting and the dialogue is snappy. Basil did a beautiful job creating a life for Barabbas. It reflects scripture and is true to the message of the Gospel. In fact, "Jesus is a genius" as one of the characters in BARABBAS proclaims. Thanks, Basil for telling us the Gospel story in a fresh way. It is true that the kingdom of God is open now for any who will follow. My prayer is that you will read this story and discover for yourself that Jesus was and is still worth following.

*Rev. Roberta Mosier-Peterson, Pastor, Oakdale Free Methodist Church*

Thoroughly enjoyable! Basil Clark humanizes a Bible character who is mentioned in only two passages of Scripture. His work of fiction portrays Barabbas as Everyman, and Mr. Clark not only provokes thought about this historically notorious character, but mediation as well, as we identify not only with Barabbas, but a character whose name has become synonymous with betrayal, Judas Iscariot. This work is not only insightful and an eye-opener to Jewish life under Roman oppression, but it is extremely entertaining as well.

*David Ramey, Evangelist and Teacher*

BARABBAS radiates with familiarity in situations we can relate to while giving us a story about hope and change. This book forces us to look at Barabbas more deeply, being propelled beyond our first thoughts. The story reminds me how truly remarkable our Savior is, and of our many second chances we receive. What a wonderful book!

*Stephanie Daniels, Ooltewah, Tennessee*

# DEDICATION

Many authors dedicate a book to their spouse.
Now I know why.
To Cora, my loving wife, for invaluable feedback,
continual support and motivation,
and for the final proofreading.
We have so much fun just being together.

# ACKNOWLEDGEMENTS

I thank Sherry Marrs, Cathy Thornsbury,
James Browning, Mike McGill, and Elgin Ward
for proofreading and feedback.

# TABLE OF CONTENTS

Barabbas, Son of a Father

x

# FOREWORD

He is a man with unique gifts; you could say he is a man of multiple talents. This is my neighbor, Professor Basil Clark.

During June of 2010, Basil gave me a copy of his book, "Poetic Healing". In his book, I saw a man with a passionate love of writing. "Poetic Healing" is a book about relationships that will consume you, motivate you, and change your very life. God has allowed Basil and me to have a wonderful relationship as neighbors.

The days of January 10th and 11th, 2011 had produced an eight-inch blanket of snow. On January 11th I was shoveling the snow from my driveway when I heard Basil call my name. Looking around I saw that he had his snow shovel in hand; ready to help me remove the snow from my driveway. This writer not only writes about relationships, he acts out relationships.

It was during this time, while shoveling the snow that we stopped to rest a moment. During the next few moments together he began to share with me the short story of Barabbas he was writing.

As he shared with me his ideas, I knew that some of the short story was scriptural, and factual, while other parts were mindful fiction. I had learned by reading "Poetic Healing" that Basil could bring what he was sharing with me into a wonderful story about Barabbas. As we began to shovel snow again, I could feel excitement with the opportunity that I would have to read his finished product about Barabbas.

*Barabbas* is a fascinating story with insight into how changing your thinking will change your emotions. We know that the elongated fictional life of Barabbas in the story did not happen, for the most part, but who am I to say it did not? It is possible God gave Basil a spiritual insight into the past so that somehow people reading this story might have their life changed. As I sat in my den, having just finished reading the final draft of Barabbas, I could not contain my emotions. I began to weep and began to think, "Could it have been this way?" My prayer is that those who might be identified as a Barabbas of today will read this story and be consumed by it and that their life will be changed.

*Bishop Don Glenn, Ordained Bishop, Church of God, Cleveland, TN*
*Presiding Bishop, International Congress of Churches and Ministries*

# PREFACE

In 1985 I was traveling from North Carolina to Kentucky, and as usual, my mind was off on its own little journey. It was the week before Easter, so I guess that is why my thoughts wandered that direction for a while. For some reason, Barabbas crossed my mind, and I wondered if he saw Jesus on the cross. I also wondered, *if* he did, what he thought, for *in the most literal sense*, Barabbas is the only one Jesus immediately died for. One was to be released, the other was to die. We know what happened. This also means, Barabbas, of everyone born into this world, was the only person for whom Jesus died twice.

So, if Barabbas happened to see Jesus hanging from the cross, what thoughts passed through his mind? We don't know, but that mere fact has never stopped any writer from going ahead with a story. I pulled a small notebook from my breast pocket and at 60 mph scribbled down, *"His arrest had nothing to do with me, and yet the way things have been intertwined, I wonder if I could have done things differently to avoid this."*

I knew at that point that a play was in the making, but I had no idea where I was going with it yet. A minute later, the notebook was again "in service" as I wrote: *Barabbas – "I've searched myself – I can't seem to find faith for a Messiah. I'm afraid any freedom we'll get will only be after hard work, sweat, and bloodshed."*

Then I wondered if Barabbas was married and had any children. So the idea was born that perhaps his wife wanted him to stay around the house more rather than out running after revolutions and insurrections, and/or maybe they argued a lot. So, the next part was inscribed into the notebook: *Barabbas – "Kids, I'm sure they'll be better off without me."*

The only other aspect of the play I was able to come up with at that particular time was the thought that *Barabbas* meant "Son of a Father," and that Jesus seems to have gotten into a little bit of trouble over ideas about him calling himself "Son of the Father." So I wondered about the idea that maybe we had the exchange of one Barabbas for another.

The three scribblings in the aforementioned notebook sat for several months before I tried to put some sense of direction and structure to them. About two and a half years after the initial thoughts, finally a script was typed. In 1988 I directed the play "Barabbas" at Lees College, Jackson, Kentucky. A few years later I adapted the script into a Biblical character monologue, BARABBAS, which I have performed at several churches and schools in Eastern Kentucky, North Carolina, and Missouri.

However, I kept "being prodded" by the idea of turning the monologue into a short story, and I finally came up with the context of an older Barabbas reflecting on earlier events in his life as he sits on a ledge overlooking his Bethlehem home. Now, we know some of the events depicted in this story did happen. Some did not. This is not an attempt to re-create Biblical history, but rather one to look for human elements that could have been involved in the events, and to glean for truths from an old story and perhaps look at them in a new way.

What about the person, Barabbas? Who was he? And, why, of all persons born into the world, did the life of this particular one intersect with the life of Jesus Christ on a given day in such a critical way?

So perhaps the only thing we can say about the character BARABBAS in this story *Barabbas* is, we know that it DIDN'T happen this way. One thing for which there is no historical basis is the idea that Barabbas had any contact with Jesus during the latter's three year period of ministry. However, Judas Iscariot was one of the Twelve, and we can speculate that he was the one most likely to lean more in the direction of Barabbas than any of the other disciples. So Barabbas could have been the type attracted to following Jesus, and except for mitigating circumstances, might even have been considered for discipleship as the Twelve were being chosen.

And just who is it that becomes a revolutionary, or an activist, or possibly even a preacher? Has it not sometimes been one who "received a charge" from his or her mother, or some other person with influence over his life, that "God had great things for him to do," and so this mission-complex-burdened person set out to change the world, for indeed, was that not his or her destiny?

# CHAPTER ONE
# The Messiah?

Even though it took him a little longer than it had in his younger days to climb the rocks leading to his favorite thinking spot, Barabbas liked to sit on the ledge that overlooked his hometown. He walked with a slight limp ever since a slip and fall many years back, but all the accident had done was make him climb more carefully and be even more thankful for the scene that was spread out in front of him and which could only be appreciated from that particular spot. He used his constant companions and helpers, two walking sticks, to assist in lowering himself to the rock, then leaned back against a Terebinth tree. As he gazed down over Bethlehem in the direction that afforded a view of his lifetime home, Barabbas' thoughts went back in time to some things from ... almost twenty years earlier, but he remembered them like they had occurred just the day before. His journey started the day he had joined his friend Judas Iscariot at the edge of a large crowd. Judas stood out in the crowd; he was taller than most of the other men, with dark hair and beard, and piercing brown eyes.

And the first thing Judas said to Barabbas was, "You're late, Barabbas."

"Like I don't already know that. I should have left the house earlier. It probably would have avoided a lot of trouble with Tamar."

Barabbas was known amongst his friends for saying he believed that in Proverbs, King Solomon was referring to Tamar when writing that "a quarrelsome wife was like a constant dripping." Barabbas felt like Tamar was against anything he wanted to do. He felt it was important to be involved in resistance to the Roman government, and Tamar was always complaining that he should spend more time at his trade as a leather-worker. Barabbas argued back that the more he earned the more she wanted to spend at the marketplace. And, whenever he mentioned to Judas he thought he might see if he could find a Rabbi who would help him find grounds for divorcing Tamar, Judas would always say, "But Barabbas, what about the prophet Malachi and what he had to say about divorce?"

Barabbas' standard response was, "Malachi! Ha! Malachi did not have to live with my wife." But, the reason Barabbas was joining Judas that particular day had nothing to do with Tamar; they were going to listen to a new prophet called John the Baptist. Some said the Baptist claimed the Messiah was coming soon. Barabbas thought it would be nice if the prophet was right because it was time the Jewish men again took charge of their land, and their homes.

As they worked their way through the crowd to get closer to the prophet, a few people protested. "Where do you think you're going?" one man snarled as he pushed Barabbas to the side. Barabbas clenched his fists, and then decided not to take a swing. Away from you, he thought as he moved to his left and continued forward.

When he and Judas were close enough to see John the Baptist, Barabbas decided John looked pretty much as he had pictured him: medium build, unkempt beard and hair, wearing a leather loincloth. Barabbas had heard some people say he looked like Elijah resurrected.

But now that they were within hearing distance of John the Baptist, Barabbas wasn't sure how well he understood the message. John spoke in a thundering voice, "And so I say to you, look inside. You say that there is trouble in the land? Trouble in the homes? I tell you that the land and the homes do not produce trouble. Look inside yourselves and repent for the kingdom of heaven is near. Some of you may be saying to yourselves, or maybe even saying to others, 'If only the Romans were not in Israel', or perhaps you may be saying, 'If only my wife were different' ..."

Barabbas turned to Judas. "Well, I definitely agree with the prophet on the last two statements, especially 'if only my wife were different'."

But then the Baptist raised his right hand, and, pointing skyward with his index finger, went on to say, "If these are your thoughts then I tell you, you are deceiving yourself because those are not the thoughts of repentance. The priests offer the blood of animals as a sin offering in the holy place, but the bodies are burned outside the city in the dump, in the unholy place." John the Baptist's voice grew even louder. "True repentance means being willing to admit that you are in the unholy place, that you are the one in the wrong."

"What?" one of the priests hollered. "You must be crazy! We Jewish people have endured suffering while waiting for Messiah, and you want to tell us that we are the ones in the wrong?"

Barabbas also stiffened. His wife Tamar might have gone along with what the Baptist was saying, but Barabbas agreed with the priest.

And then to top it off, John replied, "Suffering? A proud suffering! But your lives do not produce fruit in keeping with repentance. You think that because Abraham is your ancestor that everything is okay with you. But God does not care who your ancestors are, or what they did. He cares about what you do and who you are becoming. I tell you, the day is coming when every tree that does not produce good fruit will be cut down and thrown into the fire."

The priest angrily gestured as he talked to those around him. "Prophet? What are people thinking when they call this man a prophet?"

"Well," Barabbas laughingly said to Judas, "something must be bothering John the Baptist for him to be talking so harshly to the crowd. It sounds like maybe John had a rough morning with his wife, too, and now he's taking it out on everyone else."

"I've heard the Baptist isn't married," Judas replied.

John pointed to the river Jordan as he said, "I baptize with water, but someone is coming after me who will baptize with the Holy Spirit and fire."

"I'm not real sure what the prophet means by that, but it does look like he's making more priests angry. Look at their faces, Judas!"

John continued. "True worship of the God who made the universe takes place in spirits and thoughts and attitudes, not in your temples or traditions! Those are made by man, and if you trust in them you are no different than those who worship idols!"

"You know," Barabbas said to Judas, "he sounds a bit revolutionary and I like that. But Judas, it sounds as if the Baptist is against the Jewish authorities as much as the Romans."

"I figure," Judas replied, "the prophet will be lucky if the priests don't have him arrested."

**Barabbas shifted his position against the Terebinth tree. He remembered well how upset the priests had become if they felt that anyone was trying to usurp their religious authority. And it was just as true now as it was then. As he watched an eagle circle overhead, again Barabbas drifted back to twenty years earlier.**

John went on. "People, if you will accept the truth, he will set you free."

"What do you mean," one of the priests angrily challenged, "he will set us free?"

"The truth is alive and even now walks among you," John answered. He pointed to the river Jordan again. "I will baptize anyone who can accept what I am saying and wants to be part of the new kingdom!"

Barabbas thought a moment about what the Baptist had just said, and then turned again to Judas. "I want to be part of the new kingdom, but I'm not so sure that John the Baptist is the way to it." Judas nodded in agreement, and Barabbas continued. "I think before any new kingdom gets established, someone is going to have to shed a little blood. Say, who's that?" Barabbas pointed to a man stepping out of the crowd and telling John to baptize him, "And what's he doing?"

"Don't know," Judas responded. "I don't know him."

"I do." A man next to them spoke.  "Funny, isn't it?"

Barabbas and Judas turned to the man who had spoken. "What is?" Judas asked.

"Funny," the man responded, "how you can grow up in the same village as someone, but you just don't get to know them."

"How's that?" Barabbas asked.

"Well, I'm from Nazareth, grew up just a few houses from Jesus. That's his name. But I seldom saw him. Of course, he spent most of his time either in his father's carpenter shop, talking to the Rabbis, or, according to my mother, taking walks and talking with his mother."

Barabbas shrugged and turned back to hear the conversation between this Jesus and the prophet, but it sounded like a bunch of riddles. John was saying, "Me baptize you? Jesus, it is you who should be baptizing me." John again raised his voice as he addressed the crowd. "People," he said, "listen to this man! It is he of whom I am speaking!" John seemed to be saying Jesus was the truth that was alive and walking among them, but that didn't make any sense to Barabbas. There seemed to be nothing about Jesus that made him stand out. He appeared to be about the same age as Barabbas, thirty, and wasn't particularly comely or handsome in appearance.

**The eagle was still gliding in wide circles. Every time he saw one Barabbas thought it would be a wonderful feeling to be able to fly, but he knew there were some things that were never meant to be. A human flying was one of those things. He gave a wistful smile and returned to his memories.**

"It is not my time yet." Jesus told John and then added, "I must fulfill the righteousness of the law."

John paused. "All right, Jesus, I will baptize you, but I don't understand why."

Jesus smiled. "Cheer up, John. If you want to be a true follower of me, there will be a lot of things you don't understand. Have you looked at a small baby lately?"

Barabbas thought it was a rather strange question to ask someone and told Judas that if John the Baptist had looked at any babies lately, his appearance had probably frightened them. John the Baptist must have also thought it a strange question; his eyebrows furrowed as he scratched his ear. He looked questioningly at Jesus as he said, "Of course, I have, and I think babies are quite remarkable little miracles. Why do you ask?"

"Well, miracles they are, yes, but they come about as the result of certain laws already in effect in the universe. And, a difficult concept to understand, John, but they start from thoughts. And this is the start of the growth of a new thought, a new idea in the world, a light that can never be put out."

Barabbas was trying to comprehend what Jesus meant by saying babies started from thoughts. He turned to Judas Iscariot. "I'm having trouble understanding what Jesus and John are talking about because of all them riddles."

Judas crossed his left arm over his stomach so his left fist could support his right elbow. He raised his right arm so his chin rested against his right thumb and his forefinger extended across his pursed lips. "Maybe they aren't riddles," he said. "Maybe it's symbolic talk so they can't be accused of trying to overthrow the Roman government."

Barabbas thought there was a lot of merit in that idea and excitedly replied, "You know, Judas, you may be on to something! Let's keep track of these men. This just may be the revolution we have been looking for!" He continued, "And, if you are right about it all being symbolic talk, it is a neat idea they have, talking in code. This sounds like it could be exciting!"

Judas drew in a deep breath. Ever since he had been a young boy listening to the men of the village debate over whether or not the Messiah would come in their lifetime, he had dreamed of being a leader in a revolution. "Well, I'm ready," he said, "and so are my swords. Say, why don't we try and meet with John the Baptist and Jesus privately to see if maybe we can get into the core of the group. Maybe we can get some positions of leadership, so when the revolution is over we can be part of the ruling class."

That sounded good to Barabbas; "But," he reminded Judas, "Even if Jesus and John the Baptist are modern day Maccabeus brothers, they won't want any uprising to eventually end as Judas Maccabeus and Simon Thassi's did, in futility. Plus," Barabbas added, "We really don't even know if this is the beginning of any revolution."

Judas rolled his eyes and shook his head at Barabbas. "We'll never know unless we check it out more."

"True. So when should we try to get up with them?"

"How about tomorrow?"

"Sounds good to me," Barabbas replied.

"Then I'll be by your house around midday."

"I'll be ready."

"I doubt it," Judas said, "but I'll be there at midday anyway."

Barabbas stood slowly with the use of his wooden companions. Although he thoroughly enjoyed being at this spot, his arthritis made it necessary for him to move around every so often. He walked to the edge of the overlook and leaned heavily against his walking sticks. He'd had them both for about twenty-five years. Both were branches carved from a Terebinth tree; one was covered with an Israeli viper snakeskin. Barabbas thought of the day he had encountered this particular snake right outside the door of his dwelling. The vipers were quite poisonous, though not overly aggressive. They did, however, not like being disturbed, and, if they were, would hiss loudly. Barabbas liked to joke to his friends that upon spotting the viper, he had

had two thoughts go through his mind. "First," he would say, "I figured he wanted something to do, and second, I figured he was lonely and wanted a companion." Then Barabbas would hold the stick up. "So I solved both his problems. He's helped me travel many, many miles, and since he's always by my side, he's no longer lonely."

# CHAPTER TWO
## Life's not Fair!

**Barabbas shifted weight on his sticks again, looked down at the way he had earlier climbed, and smiled in recollection of what was, at the time, an extremely painful experience.**

Tamar had long, dark hair that came halfway down her back, and a pretty oval-shaped face with dark eyes that flashed challenge, especially to Barabbas. Around midday she heard knocking and answered the door to find Judas standing there. He was on time as he had promised Barabbas the day before. However, Barabbas was unable to go with his friend to talk with Jesus and the prophet.

"Judas, come on in," Tamar said, "Barabbas is expecting you."

Judas smiled as he stepped through the doorway. "But he's not ready to go yet, right?"

Tamar laughed and rolled her eyes upward. "I'll let him tell you himself."

Judas saw Barabbas sitting with his leg heavily wrapped, and asked, "What happened to you?"

"Well, I decided to take a walk after I got home yesterday, just thinking about some of the things we heard, and while climbing those rocks up to what you know is ..."

"Your favorite thinking spot," Judas laughed.

"He slipped and fell," Tamar added.

"And," Barabbas rolled his eyes sideways at his wife, "anyway, I think I broke a leg."

"I'm really sorry," Judas said, "and it looks like you won't be moving around very much, or going anywhere, for quite a while."

Tamar's eyes flashed. "I always tell him he should be more careful," she interjected, "but does he ever listen to me?" She said her next word slowly and sarcastically as she raised her arms, palms upward, "No…o…o…o!"

Barabbas also opened his palms upward as he said to Judas, "See what I'm going to have to listen to? Not really my concept of a revolution."

Judas laughed. He visited with Barabbas for a while, but then said that although he would like to stay and talk some more, he would have to be on his way if he was going to have any chance of talking to Jesus and John the Baptist.

"Well make sure," Barabbas told Judas, "you don't forget to mention to Jesus and John that I won't be off my leg too long, and that I really would like to be a part of the group."

"I won't forget," Judas said as he turned to leave.

After Judas was gone Tamar said, "I sure hope you're not off your leg too long. You need to get back to work in the leather-shop."

~~~

A couple hours later Barabbas painfully moved out to the doorway of his house and watched his three children playing. Deborah, age 12, looked a lot like him with dark, olive colored skin and dark brown piercing eyes. Her hair was like Tamar's, long and dark, also coming halfway down her back. Joshua, age 10, had the same dark skin and hair, but his eyes were a lighter shade of brown. Tirzah, age 6, looked exactly like her mother, a pretty oval-shaped face with the dark eyes that flashed challenge. While Barabbas was standing there, one of his neighbors, Hizkiah Bar Zalmon, stopped by to see how he was doing.

"Barabbas," he sighed, shaking his head, "I believe I have told you before, you need to be more careful climbing those rocks. We're not old men yet, but we're not fifteen, either."

"I don't need you to remind me of that," Barabbas joked.

Hizkiah laughed as he pointed at the wrap on Barabbas' leg, "I guess not anymore."
~~~

"Maybe you can get him to listen," Tamar said as she joined them. He sure doesn't pay any attention to what I offer in the way of guidance."

Hizkiah shook his head. "I doubt if I can get anything through to Barabbas. Even as young boys playing, he wouldn't take my advice." He turned to Barabbas and grinned. "By the way, Barabbas, I do want to be a good neighbor; if there is any way I can help, let me know."

"I appreciate that, but, at the moment I can't think of anything. But I will let you know if there is. So far Tamar has been having the children go to the butcher shop and take care of a few other things."

Hizkiah smiled. "Children; in the words of the Psalmist, a gift from God; they are his reward. A fact we realize in times like this, perhaps even a little more."

Barabbas grimaced as he shifted position, and then answered. "Some. Of course, Hizkiah, you have been truly blessed. I mean, look at you. Your firstborn is a son, not like me." Tamar's jaws tightened as they always did whenever Barabbas started talking this way. Barabbas threw up his hands as he continued, "But, oh, no, God didn't see his way to bless me like that. Of course, I did get Joshua, my second born; at least I got him. But you, three sons, not like me; only one son."

Hizkiah had heard this talk before and he didn't quite understand it, as to him, all children were precious. "Barabbas," he reminded as he had done before, "along with Joshua you have two beautiful daughters."

"Not much there; too much like their mother," Barabbas retorted back. "They're supposed to be learning how to be wives from Tamar," he added, "and I hope that she's teaching them to be better ones than she is." Tamar bit her lip and held Tirzah and Deborah's hands.

Hizkiah was feeling very awkward and looked down at his sandals self-consciously. "Well," he said, "I hope you get to feeling better soon, and remember, if there is anything you need, let me know." As Hizkiah left, Tamar turned and went back into the house, her humiliation combined with outrage.

~~~

A little later, with the help of some crutches another neighbor had brought by for him to use, Barabbas managed to painfully make his way over to his leather-shop. The children were still playing outside when Tamar heard a knock at the door. It was Keren, one of her neighbors. Keren had naturally-curly, black shoulder-length hair, a rounded chin, and a small, slightly upturned nose. Tamar told her it was good to see her, and invited her in.

"Tamar, my husband told me what happened yesterday."

"Yes, thank goodness your Jonathan was out walking near the rocks."

"My husband told me he saw Barabbas slip and fall," Keren told Tamar, "and while rushing to him, had feared the worst."

Tamar thoughtfully shook her head as she replied. "Well, it was a good thing Jonathan was there, as I don't think Barabbas could have made it home without his help."

"My husband thinks Barabbas' leg might be broken," Keren said. "Do you?"

Tamar's voice raised a little as she replied. "I probably shouldn't say this, but I almost hope so, so that maybe that man will learn something and be more careful. Of course, the bad part now is I will have to wait on him hand and foot, and, trust me, he is not an easy man to please."

Keren patted Tamar's shoulder, "Please, if you need any help let me know. I'll do everything I can."

"Thank you," Tamar said.

"You're welcome," Keren replied. "I have to go," she added. "I just wanted to let you know you should feel free to call on me if necessary."
~~~

As Keren was leaving, another neighbor, Hizkiah's wife, Priscilla, was approaching the door. Priscilla was more fair-skinned than most Jewish women, and had lighter brown eyes that appeared to be always smiling. "I'm just leaving to go to market," Keren told Priscilla, "but I'm sure Tamar will welcome your visit."

Tamar was at the door and said, "I most certainly will."

Priscilla warmly greeted Tamar with a hug. "How are you doing? My husband said Barabbas hurt his leg."

Tamar rolled her eyes as she replied. "Barabbas should expect to get hurt as he seems to think he's still a young boy, climbing rocks all the time."

As she sat down, Priscilla responded. "Hizkiah laughed about Barabbas still climbing; said they used to climb those rocks often as boys; that it was a beautiful view, but one he was just going to remember anymore."

"It is a pretty spot," Tamar smiled in recollection, "I'll grant you that. Before we had Deborah, I climbed it with Barabbas once. But you know, you have to quit doing some things once you have children. But, no, not Barabbas. He calls it his thinking spot. I wish he'd think a little more about working in his leather-shop. Thinking! All he wants to think about is chasing after rumors of revolution and insurrection."

Priscilla looked down and rested her chin against her smallest finger and thumb as her other fingers went up against her cheek. "There seems to be enough of that kind of talk going around these days."

Tamar shook her head. "I think sometimes that half the men never grow out of their boyhood games of playing David and Goliath."

"Or Gideon against the Philistines," Priscilla added.

Tamar laughed as she continued with, "Jepthah against the Ammonites."

Priscilla raised her head and cocked it sideways as she said, "I guess I'm lucky, because Hizkiah doesn't dream of being a revolutionary guerrilla."

"What I wonder," Tamar said, "is if boys are going to dream of accomplishing something great, why don't they dream of being a leader like Solomon was? I recall the Rabbi saying once that during King Solomon's reign there were forty years of peace."

Priscilla laughed as she replied, "I can agree with the forty years of peace part, but, for the sake of our girls, I'm not so sure we would want our boys dreaming about growing up being another Solomon."

"Why do you say that?"

Priscilla threw up her hands. "Three hundred wives and seven hundred concubines? I'm curious as to where that would leave the girls they take as wives."

"Just another face in the crowd." Tamar agreed.

"But anyway," Priscilla said, "I came to see how you're doing. I imagine with Barabbas' leg hurt you have to do a little more work."

Tamar sighed. "He's not an easy man to care for, that's for sure."

Priscilla gave a somewhat sad smile. She had been friends with Tamar since childhood, and she knew that Tamar was not happy in her marriage. "If I can help with the children in any way, let me know."

"Thanks," Tamar replied. She pursed her lips in a crooked manner and gave a little snort. "Those are words I'll never hear Barabbas say."

"What's that?"

Tamar again sighed. "If I can help with the children in any way, let me know."

"I'm lucky there, too, with Hizkiah; that he loves doing things with the children, from taking walks, to telling them stories, to play-wrestling with them."

Tamar's eyes suddenly flashed with anger as she spurted out, "I get so upset with Barabbas sometimes, the way he puts down the girls! They're getting older; starting to understand his negative comments more. Just a little while ago Deborah asked me why her father didn't like her. How do I answer that?"

"Can you talk to Barabbas? Tell him what Deborah said? Maybe if he knew how Deborah was feeling he might be more careful with his words. But, anyway," she added, "I really need to be going; I just wanted to make sure you know you can feel free to ask for help if you need any."

"Thanks, Priscilla, and trust me, I am just waiting for the time to talk to Barabbas about the way he talks about the girls; he will definitely hear from me. But it's not like it will do any good;" Tamar added, "like he ever listens to me."

Priscilla wished her good luck and reiterated that if Tamar needed any help with the children, or for that matter, with anything, to just let her know. Tamar said she would, and hugged Priscilla as she thanked her again.

~~~

About a week after Barabbas injured his leg, Judas visited again. Tamar greeted him and let him in.

"So," Judas asked, turning toward Barabbas, "How's the leg doing?"

"Good as can be expected, I guess. So what news do you have for me?"

"That's it? No 'Hello, Judas. How are you?'"

"Sorry. How is it going?"

"I'm doing well. Just harassing you. By the way, the reason I'm here, along with checking on how your leg is, is because I do have some real good news. Jesus is going to have his own group in preparation for a new kingdom, and he is going to have an inner group of twelve." Judas excitedly continued. "And I've been chosen to be
~~~

a part of them!" Judas continued telling Barabbas several things he had talked about with Jesus.

"Well, I'm glad for you," Barabbas said, "but I guess you know I'm a bit upset over my fall. It couldn't have come at a worse time."

"You can still help the group." Judas told him. "Whenever any of them are working in this area, you can provide food and lodging."

"Big deal," Barabbas caustically replied as he threw his hands up, "Serving a meal and providing a bed. What does that have to do with a revolution?"

"May I remind you Barabbas, that if you were thinking clearly and not bitterly, you would realize, would you not, that the Roman soldiers would have it a lot more difficult if they didn't quarter themselves in Jewish homes and fill their bellies at Jewish tables?"

Barabbas raised his voice as he replied. "I know that, Judas, but when it comes to the revolution I would really like to be a bigger player, do something a little more meaningful!"

"It's just not fair," Barabbas said as he painfully pulled himself up from the table, leaned heavily on his walking sticks, and limped over to where he could look out at the ledge where he liked to reflect. He realized Judas was correct; he was thinking bitterly. He further realized he didn't care. "I sure wish I could have talked to Jesus before I broke my leg. Maybe he would have also selected me as one of the Twelve."

"You'd fit for sure," Judas nodded in agreement. "So far we are a rather rough bunch. You remember Simon Bar Jonas?"

Barabbas jerked around quickly and winced as pain shot up his leg. "That hotheaded fisherman!" he shouted. "No!" Judas shrugged. "Then again," Barabbas calmed down some as he continued, "I don't know. If this Jesus is as good as you say he is, I guess he can keep Bar Jonas in line. But I can't imagine Simon not constantly being in an argument with someone." Another thought struck him. "But, who knows, on the other hand, maybe the very reason Jesus chose him for the group is because he is so good at stirring up trouble."

Judas chuckled as he said, "Jesus told Bar Jonas from this point on he will be known as Simon Peter, or, the Rock."

"So what about John the Baptist?"

"I'm not sure why," Judas said, "but John is not going to be one of the Twelve. As a matter of fact, just yesterday I heard someone ask John about the fact that so many of his followers are leaving him and going with Jesus, and John just smiled and said, 'You yourselves can testify I said, I am not the Messiah, but am sent ahead of him. The friend who attends the bridegroom waits and listens for him, and is full of joy when he hears the bridegroom's voice. That joy is mine, and it is now complete. This is the way it is supposed to be; I, John, must decrease and Jesus must increase'."

Barabbas cocked his head a little to one side as he told Judas, "That seems rather strange; I would think as fiery as John is, he would be the main assistant to Jesus. But anyway," he continued, "did you talk to Jesus about holding a spot for me in the Twelve until my leg gets better?"

Judas scrunched his lips a bit sideways before he replied. "Yes, but I'm not so sure Jesus makes that decision on his own."

"What makes you say that?"

Judas shrugged. "His father must be involved in some way. Jesus said he did nothing without his father's approval. They must have some sort of spying system because Jesus knows secret things about everyone he has selected to be in the Twelve.

"Do you think Jesus can think for himself?"

"I don't know, but from the way John the Baptist talked the day we first heard him at the river Jordan, it does sound like something major is underway."

**Barabbas smiled down again over the rocks that had so impacted his life and then moved away from the edge of the**

**overlook, sat back down, and leaned back again against the Terebinth.**

Several weeks after the conversation with Judas, Barabbas' leg was feeling somewhat better and he was managing to get around fairly well. One evening when Judas and Thomas were working in the area they stopped in to spend the night with him. *Thomas*, Barabbas thought, *Why Jesus chose him, I don't know. Myself, I have serious doubts about Thomas, serious doubts.* After Barabbas welcomed his guests into his home and saw they had something to eat and drink, he asked Judas what was going on.

Judas replied, "I hate to be so blunt, but it doesn't look so good."

Barabbas leaned forward into the table. "What's wrong? Are the Romans causing problems?"

Judas took a deep breath, started to pucker his lips, and then sighed before replying. "I wish it was the Romans. We expect trouble from them, but it really hurts when it comes from your own kind."

Barabbas had a puzzled look on his face as he asked, "What do you mean by that, Judas?"

"King Herod had John the Baptist arrested."

"What for? I thought he liked, or at least, tolerated him."

"Probably under pressure from his new wife, Herodias," Judas replied.

"That doesn't surprise me too much," Barabbas laughed, "someone having trouble from his wife, even if he is the king." Barabbas realized it gave him a certain satisfaction being aware of that commonality as he asked Judas, "But why would Herodias want John the Baptist arrested?"

"Well, about a week ago John hollered out to Herod from a crowd it was unlawful for him to have his own brother's wife. Herodias was with him, and visibly upset. Actually," Judas continued, "people who observed the incident said it was obvious Herodias was furious at the Baptist."

"I think she wants him put to death," Thomas added.

"Well," Barabbas said, "that will sure put the king in a tight spot; John the Baptist is quite popular with many of the common people throughout the land, and Herod knows it. If he puts John to death there will be a lot of trouble. It will divide the people, and in my opinion, we Jews need to be sticking together now more than ever if we are going to have any chance of overthrowing the Romans." Barabbas sighed. "I guess we'll just have to wait and see what happens."

The last time Barabbas talked with Judas he had asked him about seeing if Jesus might save a place in the Twelve until his leg got better. Now he figured he could start putting longer distances on it in the next few days, so he asked Judas, "What about the Twelve? Is Jesus going to save me a spot?"

"I put in a good word for you," Judas told Barabbas, "and I hate to tell you this, but just yesterday Jesus told Matthew the tax collector he could join us, and, unfortunately for you, that fills the twelfth position."

Astonishment and anger overwhelmed Barabbas as he quickly stood up. "Matthew the tax collector! He has been working for the Romans!" Barabbas moved to the window where he could view his thinking spot in the distance. "What in the world is your Jesus thinking of?"

Judas leaned back against the rear of his chair. "I don't know, but the thing bothers me is that Jesus designated me as the treasurer for our group, and with that crooked tax collector along, who knows what might happen? I'm even wondering if Jesus might be thinking of turning over the finances to Matthew because of his experience with money. I mean, why else would he recruit him? If that is the case, " Judas added, "I will have to give serious consideration to dropping out."

"I doubt that," Thomas laughed. "I don't think you're leaving anytime soon."

"What makes you say that?" Judas retorted.

"I see that look in your eyes. You like revolutionary ideas."

Judas leaned forward on the table and rested his chin in the palms of his hands. He looked down at the table, then back to Thomas and shrugged. "Yeah, you're probably right."

"Well, since we're on the topic of money," Barabbas asked Judas, "how have donations been?"

"It's funny," Judas replied, "but Jesus does seem to have some sort of strange appeal to a few women with rich husbands."

"Even Suzanna," Thomas interjected.

"Suzanna?" Barabbas knew of a couple women named Suzanna.

"Yes," Thomas excitedly continued, "the one whose husband is a captain for King Herod. She has said she will give regularly to the cause."

Barabbas turned his head quickly in surprise. The statement caught him off guard. "I really don't see her husband being in favor of revolutions or insurrections."

"Talking in code is the best part of the whole plan," Judas added. "People give as though we were some sort of ministry."

"Well," Barabbas responded, shaking his head, "from everything I have been hearing, it does sound as though Jesus is more concerned with healing the sick, and even playing with the children, than he is with waging a war against Rome."

"This is the beauty of the whole plan," Thomas said.

Barabbas squinted questioningly. "How's that?"

"Because it looks like Jesus is building a strong support base without arousing the suspicions of Rome." Thomas continued, "Barabbas, you have got to meet Jesus as soon as you can walk longer distances. I think you'll agree with me, this man is a genius."

~~~

The next day, after Judas and Thomas had departed, Tamar told Barabbas, "We need to talk."
~~~

"What now?"

"Barabbas. Not too long ago Deborah asked me why you didn't like her. I told her that it was you who had wanted to name her Deborah, after the Judge in the Scriptures. And do you know what she replied? Your daughter said, 'That doesn't mean he loves me.' I told her you do love her, that you just didn't always show it. Although," she added, "it seems a shame that I have to even tell her that."

Barabbas furrowed his brow. "What's there to show? I bring home shekels for their food."

Tamar shook her head in disbelief. "But the girls are getting older, Barabbas. They are realizing that you are not being fair with them."

"Life's not fair!" Barabbas sneered, "Otherwise I'd have had more sons!"

# CHAPTER THREE
## Paradoxes

**Barabbas stood to stretch again and gazed northeast toward Jerusalem. *Oh, Jerusalem,* he thought, *the city that changed forever the direction of my life.* He shifted his weight on his walking sticks as he thought about his first time talking with Jesus. It sure hadn't turned out the way he thought it might.**

About a month after Judas and Thomas spent the night with him, Barabbas decided his leg was well enough to make the five-mile trip to Jerusalem where Jesus was speaking to the people and teaching on an almost daily basis.

"Barabbas, it is five miles away. That's ten miles total," Tamar said. "I think you should wait a while longer."

"Even though you are good at adding numbers," Barabbas retorted, "you have no idea what my leg feels like."

"Well if it feels good enough to walk to Jerusalem, then it ought to be good enough to spend the day where you really belong, in your shop!"

"Or, on the road to Jerusalem. You don't get it, do you?"

Tamar threw her hands up in exasperation as she countered, "If you insist! I guess you are the one who knows it all!"

"I know this much," Barabbas angrily retorted. "King Solomon was correct in his writings about argumentative women."

"And just what does that have to do with walking ten miles on a leg that is not fully healed?"

"A nagging pain in my leg or a nagging sound in my ears; what does it matter? One good reason to go is to get away from the constant dripping of your quarrelsome voice." Tamar surprisingly didn't say anything back but her jaws tightened and her eyes simmered with hurt and anger.

A couple of miles later as his leg was throbbing, Barabbas wondered about the wisdom of his choice, but pride kept him from turning back home. He gripped his walking sticks, set his jaws, and kept on toward Jerusalem.

Fortunately for Barabbas, Jesus was speaking on the southern side of Jerusalem, so Barabbas' journey was a little shorter. As he approached the crowd he heard Judas Iscariot calling, "Barabbas! Over here!"

"Good. I was hoping to find you. How is it going?"

"I'm doing well. How is the leg?"

"Let's just say that if I didn't have my walking sticks, I don't think I could have made it."

"Well, I'm glad you did. Let's move in a little closer, where you can hear Jesus better."

Someone next to them called out Jesus' name,

"Who's that?" Barabbas asked.

"Eleazar, one of John the Baptist's disciples."

"Eleazar," Jesus said, "Good to see you. By your tone of voice when you called my name, I surmise you have a question for me. But first, let me ask you one. Did your parents name you after Eleazar Avaran, or Eleazar the ninety-year-old scribe who went willingly to the torture wheel rather than eat pork?"

Eleazar appeared surprised at the question, but his face beamed as he answered, "As a matter of fact, when I was a boy my parents said they named me after Eleazar Avaran. How did you know?"

"I didn't, but I like to analyze why people have certain names. Sometimes it's a family name, but other times it's after someone in history. Your parents probably hoped you would display the same courage Avaran did as he fought with his brother, Judas Maccabeus. And, actually, in days soon to come, you will need that same courage as a follower of John the Baptist."

Eleazar somberly nodded his head. "John has indicated as much."

"On a slightly lighter note," Jesus added, smiling, "I hope you don't depart this life with an elephant falling on top of you."

Eleazar laughed. "I agree. I'll try to avoid stabbing any elephants from underneath."

"So, anyway," Jesus asked, "what do you want to know?"

"John wants to know if you are who he thinks you are, or should he tell the people to be waiting for someone else?"

Jesus was quiet for several seconds, and then said, "Go back to John and tell him what you see and hear here today, that those with skin afflictions are healed, the blind receive their sight, the crippled walk, and the deaf hear. Tell him I preach the message of good news to the poor. And, also tell him I would love to release him from prison, but that is not what I sense the Father would have me do." Jesus paused, and then added, "Tell John not to give up hope, for the kingdom of heaven is advancing, but not without violent men taking hold of it."

Barabbas liked the latter part of what Jesus said and turned to Eleazar. "You know, I think Jesus is right. Maybe we ought to have some violence now; maybe a little riot would pressure King Herod to release the prophet in an attempt to keep things calm; to keep the Romans from intervening."

"Exactly what I told John, but he said the kingdom of heaven was not to enter in by way of sword."

Barabbas tried to clarify things in his mind. "Jesus," he called out above the murmur of the crowd, "didn't you just say the kingdom would not enter in without violent men taking hold of it?"

"Good question Barabbas," Jesus replied. Barabbas was startled Jesus had called him by name, but quickly surmised Jesus had assumed who he was as he was standing by Judas, and Judas had assured him that Jesus had been made aware Barabbas was interested in the group of Twelve. Jesus continued, "There will be blood shed in establishing the kingdom, but it won't come from the people. My father does not want it that way." Jesus raised his voice as he went on. "People, listen! No one ever born into this world is greater than John the Baptist, but the paradox is, someone who is least in the kingdom is greater than John."

**Barabbas shifted his weight again on his walking sticks and decided to sit back down again. Carefully he eased his aching bones to the ground and leaned back against the tree. He gazed up at some large, fluffy clouds, drew in a breath through his nose, slightly opened his lips, and released a sigh of contentment. There was a slight breeze blowing, and he wondered about the connection between it and the movement of the clouds. *So many riddles in the world,* he thought, *So many riddles.* He drifted back to Jesus' words about John the Baptist.**

*Riddles,* Barabbas thought, *Just like that day with John at the river Jordan. I can't figure out what he means.*

Then Jesus spoke again to Eleazar. "Tell John he will soon be free, and his freedom will involve more than he can even begin to comprehend right now. Tell him he will be at peace with the father."

Barabbas felt excitement surge through his body. "There he goes again," he said to Judas, "talking in the code. It sure sounds like some sort of big struggle is about to start!" *Is it possible,* Barabbas thought, *that a turning point in history is about to occur, and I may have a chance to be a part of it?* He decided to ask Jesus about something he had occasionally pondered over throughout the years. "Jesus," he asked, "do you believe that during this life God has assigned us unique tasks to accomplish – tasks he has given no one else?"

~~~

There was a knock on the door, and when Tamar called out, "Come in!" Keren and Priscilla entered.
~~~

"How are you doing?" Tamar asked them.

"Fine," Keren said "although the children are keeping me rather busy."

"You have that one right," Priscilla agreed, "and, although I know Solomon wrote in his collection that 'children are a gift from God; they are his reward', it seems he forgot to mention how busy these little gifts would keep us."

Tamar laughed. "I'm in full agreement with you on that, Priscilla."

"So, Tamar," Keren interjected as they all sat at the table, "did I see Barabbas heading out in the direction of Jerusalem earlier?"

Tamar drew in a deep breath and bit her lower lip before answering. "I tried to tell him he should stay off his leg a little longer, but, no, he's got to have it his way. Of course, if he hurts it more he'll expect me to still wait on him." She drew in another deep breath and her eyes angrily flashed as she added, "Men make a decision, but we women pay the price."

Priscilla cocked her head sideways and leaned forward over the table a little. She propped her elbows on the table and rested her chin in her hands as she said, "Some men."

"Fighting again?" Keren asked.

Venom spilled over in Tamar's voice as she continued her tirade. "You want to know what he said this morning when I told him I thought he could hurt his leg again if he walked to Jerusalem? He said King Solomon was correct in his writings about argumentative women. He said, 'A nagging pain in my leg or a nagging sound in my ears, what does it matter?' He told me one reason to go to Jerusalem was to get away from the constant dripping of my quarrelsome voice."

Keren shook her head affirmatively and repressed a smile. "Fighting again."

"Barabbas might call it nagging," Tamar retorted, "but I call it trying to keep him responsible! Barabbas has already been unable to work full-time in the leather shop for several weeks now," she added, "and it seems to me that he is willing to put even that in jeopardy, and he's not really thinking about the fact that he has a family to look after!"

Priscilla uncomfortably shifted in her chair. "Tamar," she started, "I wish I knew what to tell you, but I don't."

"Same here," Keren agreed.

Tamar snorted as she said, "That's all right. There isn't much you can tell me; only Barabbas can do that."

Keren's forehead wrinkled as she quizzically raised her eyebrows. "So, Tamar just what is it that only Barabbas can tell you?"

"That he cares," Tamar said sadly. "I only want to hear from him that he wants to be with me – and the children."

~ ~ ~

"I'm sorry, Barabbas," Jesus said, "there was some other talking going on, and I didn't quite hear your full question."

Barabbas repeated, "Do you believe that during this life God has assigned us unique tasks to accomplish, tasks he has given no one else?"

"Before I answer your question," Jesus replied, "let me ask you one, Barabbas. Do you know what a paradox is?"

Barabbas shook his head. "Not really, but remember, I'm not a teacher like you."

Jesus smiled. "I love paradoxes. Something that may seem to be a contradiction, but may also be true; two things that seemingly can't coexist with each other, but there they are, side by side. For example, in the fall when leaves die and are scattered all over the ground, it looks like death has taken over and won, but what happens in the spring? Buds, new leaves, new life. Death and resurrection, hand in hand. You can't have the one without the other. Do you see that, Barabbas?"

Barabbas looked up a cloud and then back to Jesus. "I think so, but what does that have to do with my question?"

Jesus laughed. "I'm getting there; I just want to make sure you understand the paradox concept first. You see, Barabbas, the father will always find someone to do what he wants accomplished, but the paradox is, each person is unique and the only one who can perform the task set before him or her."

Barabbas scrunched his face in response to Jesus' statement, then said, "Well, Jesus, what do you think of this? I was born in Bethlehem a little over thirty years ago. My parents told me that King Herod the Great was furious over reports of a baby born that some were claiming would be a future king, so he ordered the infamous 'Bethlehem Massacre of the Innocents'. But by then my folks were visiting relatives in Hebron, and they stayed there for a while in fear of my life. So I was spared. And my mother has always told me she knows God has something special planned, some great work for me to do. What do you think of that?"

Jesus smiled as he answered. "I can identify with that situation." He then went on to say he thought Barabbas' mother was correct, but wanted to warn him of a little problem. "Whenever something of this nature is told to a young person, it becomes very easy for the child, as he or she grows up with obviously limited horizons and understandings, to misinterpret the parents and to start fantasizing about how important he or she will become. It becomes very easy for an unhealthy pride to develop. But the new kingdom is full of paradoxes; great things are found in small things; the poor in spirit will inherit the kingdom; the meek will inherit the earth; peacemakers will be called the children of God, and those who are persecuted for righteousness sake will see the kingdom of heaven. The earlier prophets who were persecuted and falsely accused have a great reward in heaven."

"All well and good," Barabbas said, shaking his head, "but this sounds like all rewards come after death. What about now?"

"Barabbas, the kingdom of heaven is righteousness, peace, and joy, and these can be found right now, on a daily basis, in day-to-day living."

"No," said Barabbas, raising his voice. "I want to know about freedom from Rome, a decent meal we don't have to work so hard for, order in our homes, and wives who will obey and help us out. What about these things?"

"Barabbas," Jesus replied, also raising his voice, "the kingdom of heaven is not meat, drink, or even freedom from political or domestic oppression. Peace and joy are available right now, under any circumstances."

Again Barabbas repeated, "No!" raising his voice even more. "I can't accept that! The kingdom of God will free us from the Romans! Jesus, don't you love your country and want freedom for our people?"

Jesus smiled and stretched his arms outward as he replied, "Barabbas, now you see through a glass darkly, but one day you will see and clearly understand. And also, remember this well, greater love hath no man than one who lays down his life for his friend."

Barabbas cocked his head sideways and then looked at Judas. "I think I understand this," he said, "This is what goes on in wars and revolutions." He turned back to Jesus. "Wait! Jesus, you said now I see through a glass darkly but someday it will be clear." Barabbas looked around and lowered his voice. "Of course, the code; I forgot it's not safe to talk openly. But you're among friends here, Jesus."

Jesus leaned forward and quietly spoke to Judas Iscariot and Barabbas. "You don't understand, a man's enemies are often found in his own household, among those he thought he could trust." He directed his next words to Barabbas. "Go home and prepare for the new kingdom there."

Barabbas had not been thinking of the pain in his leg since arriving at the hillside where Jesus was, but now he was very aware of it at the thought of trekking all the way back to his house. But overriding even the pain was, to him, the ludicrousness of Jesus' statement. "Jesus," he started, "don't you understand? My son Joshua is barely ten, not old enough to help in a revolution, and what good are two girls and a nagging wife?"

"You speak as if your son is the most important member of your family," Jesus replied. "Next to you, of course," he wryly added. "But, remember, your girls, Deborah and Tirzah – and your wife Tamar – are people too."

A surprised look came over Barabbas' face. "How do you know the names of my daughters?"

"Judas told me about your family when he asked if I would hold a place for you as one of my disciples."

"Well, since we are speaking of my request," Barabbas asked, "why didn't you include me in the Twelve?"

"Because you are already a leader of another group."

Barabbas raised his shoulders as he turned his palms facing upwards and slightly raised his arms as he asked Jesus, "What in the world are you talking about?"

"Your family. You need to start establishing peace, righteousness, and joy with them, there, now."

Barabbas raised his right walking stick about a foot and slammed it back down as he loudly retorted, "Obviously I have not made clear my home situation to you!"

Jesus shook his head. "No; obviously," he responded, "I have not made clear to you my father's methods."

Barabbas turned sharply to Judas and winced at the pain shooting up his leg. "I told you I've had my doubts about Thomas! Thinks this man" – Barabbas jerked his index thumb in the direction of

Jesus – "is a genius; I doubt it! And here I've walked almost five miles on a bad leg just to hear him; what a waste." Barabbas turned back to Jesus. "If you ever start talking sense send a message to me by way of Judas Iscariot; he knows where I live!"

"I'll do that, Barabbas, however, my message is going to stay the same; it is your understanding that will have to change."

Barabbas rolled his eyes upward, turned angrily, and started walking through the crowd toward the road to his home, sputtering to anyone who would listen, "Revolutionary leader, John the Baptist, Messiah among us. I'm afraid we're hearing a lot of talk about dreams, and a new kingdom will require more than daydreams. We need action, riots, yes, even bloodshed, if we're ever going to be free!"

Barabbas paused for a moment and behind him he could hear Jesus saying, "Freedom, we all seek it. And I tell you, you will know the truth, and the truth will set you free!"

~~~

**Barabbas shifted his legs and looked up at the moving clouds again as he recalled what happened next.**

On the way back to his house the throbbing pain in his leg escalated, but, as after his argument with Tamar, pride prevented him from turning back and asking Judas if he could spend the night with him. Instead, Barabbas gripped his walking sticks more tightly, set his jaws, and kept on toward his village. He finally arrived home after dark, and when he came through the door Tamar said, "Barabbas. I'm glad you made it back. How's your leg?"

"I don't want to talk about it," Barabbas snapped back, "I want something to eat." Tamar brought him some wine and a small loaf of bread.

"I'll have fish and more bread ready soon. Rest, and I'll hurry."

"You should have had something ready when I got home."
~~~

Tamar drew a deep breath through her nostrils. "How can I have something ready for when you get home when I never know when you are going to be here?" Barabbas clenched his teeth and stared at Tamar, his eyes warning he did not want to hear anything else.

The next day Barabbas decided to ignore his throbbing leg and make his first climb since his fall, back to his thinking spot.

"Husband! What goes on in your head?" Tamar objected, "What if you slip again? Don't you realize you have family responsibilities to take care of?"

"I don't need you telling me what I can or can't do! I think I can decide for myself!"

When Tamar saw her husband's mind was set, she sneered, "Then just go on up there; see if you can hurt your other leg this time!"

50

# CHAPTER FOUR
## Confusion Abounds!

**Barabbas recalled his climb of twenty years ago. He smiled now, but he wasn't smiling then, and he was serious about needing to sort things out. It had been a lot more difficult climb than usual, and he did slip a couple times. However, he was determined that Tamar wasn't going to be correct about him getting hurt again. He discovered determination still had its limits.**

The next morning Barabbas could barely move.

"What's wrong?" Tamar asked.

"I'm afraid," Barabbas did not want to finish the admission to Tamar, but he did, "I'm afraid that I hurt my leg again."

Uncharacteristically, Tamar said nothing, turned, and then said back over her shoulder, "I'll bring you something to eat."

For several more weeks Barabbas limped gingerly to the leather-shop where he tried to keep the business caught up. He decided it was a good time to involve Joshua in what would be his business someday, so during this time he started to teach his son the trade. Along with instructions in belt-making, Barabbas also passed on stories told to him by his father as they had worked together. Although Barabbas wouldn't admit he was doing it, he followed Tamar's advice about being careful with his leg, and avoided taking journeys away from Bethlehem for several months. Judas Iscariot visited infrequently and Barabbas eagerly listened to information on what was going on with Jesus and the Twelve. Tamar generally avoided saying anything to Barabbas about the topic, as she hoped it was just a passing phase.

~ ~ ~

When Barabbas finally went back to Jerusalem to where Jesus was again speaking to a crowd, he found Judas, and when the opportunity arose he spoke to Jesus. "Jesus, I've been thinking it over, and I really want to try and understand the code. My understanding of the scriptures is that the work of God involves bringing a new kingdom to pass. So tell me, do you have any plans of revolution against the Romans?"

"Barabbas," Jesus said, "Good to see you again. I hope your leg is finally healed, and although I think it is good to have a place to get away from others and meditate, I hope you are more careful in your climbing. Now, let's see; how to answer your question. In a few years," he went on, "there will be now unheard of things taking place within the Roman government; even some of the Roman guards will be a part of the kingdom of heaven."

Barabbas' mind reeled. He could hardly believe what he had just heard come from Jesus' mouth. "Wait a minute, Jesus. You mean you're going to take on Rome, in Rome? This kingdom is going to stretch beyond our borders?"

Jesus smiled. "You're familiar with mustard trees, I know. Well, just like a mustard tree starts from a little seed, so the seeds of the kingdom are being planted right now, and no one will be able to stop their growth."

**Barabbas looked up at the clouds again as he smiled. There had been a lot of people in the crowd that day: men, women, and children. Three women in particular had caught his attention and he had asked Judas who they were. Judas had pointed to the one who appeared to be the oldest who was wearing a light blue head cover. He told Barabbas she was Mary, the mother of Jesus, and that the other two women with her were two of her friends, Mary Magdalene and Salome. Salome looked about Barabbas' age, and Barabbas couldn't really tell about Mary Magdalene. There was something about her; she looked like she had perhaps lived a rough life, and might look a little older than she really**

**was. The three women had been talking amongst themselves, although Barabbas had not been able to make out what they were saying.**

~~~

Salome looked puzzled as she said she agreed with the man asking questions about a kingdom in Rome. "Mary," she asked, "is Jesus playing a role in the circumstances at all? I mean, I have heard some people say that Jesus is the Messiah; do you know if this is, in fact so, and, if so, is he in danger from the Romans?"

"Who my son is, is a question for him to answer, and as far as whether or not he is in danger, I hope not. However," Mary added, "my concern for him has increased ever since I heard the news of John the Baptist's arrest."

Mary Magdalene shifted her weight onto her left leg as she opened her hands and brought them together in front of her, fingers interlocking. "I also hope Jesus is not in danger," she said, and then she continued. "Salome, you know what happened to me, how Jesus forgave me, and brought me peace, when before I had a deeply troubled spirit, and no peace. When he told me my sins were forgiven he upset a lot of our religious leaders. Even now some say he is empowered by Beelzebub, the prince of demons. But I know my peace does not come from evil; it is the peace of God."

~~~

Meanwhile, Jesus gestured a welcome to three children standing close to him who looked like they might be siblings. The oldest girl looked to be about twelve, and had darker, olive colored skin, dark brown piercing eyes, and long, dark hair that came halfway down her back. The boy appeared to be about ten. He had the same dark skin and hair, but his eyes were a lighter shade of brown. The youngest girl was probably about six, and looked a lot like the oldest girl, except her face was more oval shaped. The children's clothes were ragged, and dirty.

Jesus smiled down at them. "What are your names?"

The oldest girl replied, "Sarah," the boy said, "Jonathan," and the youngest girl looked shyly at the ground. "She's Mary," Jonathan said.

"Mary. That's a pretty name." Mary quickly looked up with a smile. "As a matter of fact," Jesus added, "that's my mother's name." Mary's small face beamed.

When Jesus asked the children how they were doing, Mary just continued to smile brightly and gaze up at him. Sarah said she was fine, and Jonathan drew himself up and responded that he was doing real well. When Jesus asked them if they wanted to hear a story, they all joyfully responded "Yes!" in unison. Jesus smiled and started, "Well, once there was a shepherd who had a hundred sheep, and every night when they were coming into the fold, he counted them."

"Why did he do that?" Mary interrupted.

Jonathan shook his head and rolled his eyes. "To make sure they were all there, silly." His little sister turned red and looked down in embarrassment.

Jesus smiled and responded first to Jonathan. "That's right; to make sure they were all there." Then he reached out and took Mary's hand and drew her to him. "And you're not silly; that was a good question." Her face brightened again in response to his words. Jesus continued, "Let me ask you a question. If you had a little lamb, and you lost her, would you want to find her again?"

The little girl quickly answered, "Oh yes!" Then she glanced at her brother, but he didn't say anything to her.

"Well, one night when the shepherd was counting his sheep, instead of one hundred, there were only ninety-nine. One was missing."

Mary's eyes widened. "Oh, oh."

Jesus smiled as he responded to the interruption, "That's right, Mary, oh, oh." Then he turned to Sarah. "So, do you know what the shepherd did?"

"I think he probably went looking for it," Sarah replied. "I know I would."

"That's right!" Jesus put his arm around all of them as he went on. "And when he found it," he paused briefly as he swung Mary to his shoulders as he continued, "he joyfully put her on his shoulders and went to his friends and neighbors and said to them, 'Be happy with me; I have found my lost sheep'." Jesus looked down at Jonathan. "Do you know what that story means?"

Jonathan shrugged and turned his palms upwards as he replied, "I don't really know what it means, but I think it's a good one, and I liked it."

"I'm glad you do, and, what it means is that just like that shepherd loves his sheep, so God our father in heaven loves all of us." Jonathan nodded his head, looked up at Jesus, and then looked at his sister Mary on Jesus' shoulders, and smiled. Again, Mary shyly looked down at the ground, but this time she was not feeling chastened.

Judas turned to Barabbas and drew in his breath sharply. "This is the part about Jesus I am starting to get real frustrated with. Telling stories to kids is just wasting time we could be spending getting things ready for a revolution. What does he think, that we can wait until the boy grows up before we start anything?" Judas turned back to Jesus and called out, "Jesus, why don't you have the mothers of these children take them back to their homes so they aren't bothering you?"

All three children's faces became crestfallen, and Mary looked a little scared. Jesus swung her back down off his shoulders and held her in his arms on his right side. "Judas, don't try to stop these children from coming to me, for the kingdom of God belongs to such as these. I tell you the truth; anyone who will not receive the kingdom of God like a little child will never enter it."

A woman near them stepped forward to Jesus. "Thank you, Jesus, for taking the time for them. They don't have parents anymore, and I look out for them as much as I can. So, children, we probably really should be going. It's a long walk home, and I have to start getting supper ready." She looked down at the children. "Say goodbye to Jesus."

Sarah, Jonathan, and Mary all said goodbye, and as Jesus set Mary back down she reached up, hugged his neck, and gave him a kiss on the cheek. Then she took her surrogate mother's hand as they started to make their way out of the crowd. "I liked Jesus," Mary said, "but I didn't like that man who said we needed to go home."

"Me neither," Jonathan agreed, "especially since we really don't have one."

~ ~ ~

Judas shook his head as he spoke to Barabbas. "Got to become like a little child. What's he mean by that? You're right; the code is confusing at times."

Barabbas leaned forward putting more weight on his walking sticks. He called out to Jesus to get his attention. "Jesus," he started, "I have spent a lot of time since last talking with you thinking about this. Hard thinking, too, by the way." He laughed. "It was hard thinking because it was a lot more difficult to climb the rocks to my favorite thinking spot. But seriously, if we are about to bring a new kingdom to pass, shouldn't we be doing more than spending time with the sick and playing with the children?" Barabbas inwardly noted he was saying 'we' as if he were part of the Twelve. He realized he really did want to be a part of any insurrection that might take place. Of course, one of his earliest childhood memories was listening to the men of the village talk about the killing of Judas the Galilean, a Zealot with a small following who resisted the Roman institution of a census in order to levy taxes. But Barabbas thought a revolution could succeed with the right preparations. "I mean," he continued, "what about stockpiling swords, training soldiers, making battle plans? And what about John the Baptist in prison? What are we going to do about him?"

A look of sadness passed over Jesus' face as he replied, "John's task is done, and he has already been set free."

"The prophet is free? Where is he?"

"John has gone to a place prepared for him."

Barabbas could hardly believe how fast it looked like things were moving. Apparently Jesus was involved in a lot of work people didn't know about, and all his preaching and playing with the children was, in fact, just a cover.

"Where? In hiding?" Judas asked.

"John is safe with the father."

The words were no more out of Jesus' mouth when Eleazar rushed up and gasped, "Horrible news, Jesus! King Herod was hosting a drunken party, ordered John the Baptist beheaded, and the head delivered to the party on a platter!" The look of sadness of a moment ago returned to Jesus' face.

~ ~ ~

When Mary Magdalene heard Eleazar she gasped, "No!"

Jesus' mother, Mary, looked upward. "Dear God in Heaven, help us."

"Mary," Mary Magdalene's lips were trembling, "I'm so sorry about John."

A tear trickled down Mary's face. "I remember my first visit to my Aunt Elizabeth after I became pregnant with Jesus. My aunt was pregnant too, with John, and said she felt him leap for joy when I greeted her. I've always felt so close to John."

~ ~ ~

"Jesus," Judas challenged, "I thought you said the prophet was free, in hiding!"

"No. I said he was free, with the father."

"Jesus," Eleazar asked, "are you coming to the burial?"

"No."

"All John's followers will be there? Why not?"

"I need to spend some time alone," Jesus answered. "John is at peace now, and he will understand."

~ ~ ~

"Are you going to the burial?" Mary Magdalene asked Mary.

"Yes." She paused, and then added, "A part of me wants to go to Jesus and comfort him, but I do sense so strongly that he does need some time alone."

Mary Magdalene felt a choking in her throat as she said, "While most mothers are instinctive about what their children need, it seems, Mary, that you have insights into your son beyond most. I think you are remarkable."

"Thank you," Mary said as she sadly smiled. "And may I ask a favor of you two? Will you go with me to John's burial?"

"Of course," Mary Magdalene and Salome both agreed.

~ ~ ~

Barabbas could not believe what he had just heard, Jesus saying that John was at peace. His nostrils twitched and his body stiffened as he turned to Judas. "Look at him. No anger, nothing! You would think someone who makes claims of a coming kingdom would fight back when a leader like John the Baptist is killed! But, no, all he says is, 'Leave me alone; John is at peace; he will understand!'" Barabbas angrily swung toward Jesus. "No, Jesus! He's not at peace! His blood lies on Herod's palace floor crying out for someone to seek revenge! Why don't you do something?"

Jesus seemed calm as he answered, "Things are not always as they appear."

Jesus' calmness had the opposite effect on Barabbas as he wildly responded, "Well, some things are exactly as they appear! And it appears the prophet just lost his head! What are you going to do about that?"

Jesus again quietly replied, "I want to spend some time alone, to pray, and meditate."

Barabbas took a step toward Jesus, raised both walking sticks a little and slammed them back down as he sarcastically asked, "You call that doing something?"

Jesus stepped forward until his face was scant inches from Barabbas and then thrust his chin forward a little as he deliberately formed each word. "I call it grieving. I have just lost a cousin and a very good friend. Now if you'll allow me, I need to spend some time alone!" With that, Jesus sharply turned and walked away.

Shaken, Barabbas told Judas, "I've not seen him like this before; you know there may be some fight in him after all. It's just a matter of finding the right motivations."

**Barabbas yawned. He knew he was about to do what he had done many times before under this Terebinth tree. He scooted down so he was lying flat, turned over to his left until his stomach was in contact with and mostly facing the ground, his left leg stretched, his right leg pulled up to an almost ninety degree angle. Barabbas crooked his left arm under his face and left temple with his wrist and hand curled back so that his fingertips touched the back of his neck. It was a comfortable position for him, and he knew his nap would last about an hour. About forty-five minutes later the day had gotten hotter and sweat beaded Barabbas' forehead. He jerked awake when a fly settled on his ear. He sat up in minor confusion for a few seconds and then smiled as he saw his Israeli viper snake stick. Over twenty-five years now his walking sticks had supported him and laid beside him as he napped.**

~~~

Barabbas climbed up the rocks thinking every inch of the way of how his last conversation with Jesus had gone, and of the death of
~~~

John the Baptist. Revolution seemed inevitable; it just might need more catalyst to speed things up. However, and Barabbas hated to admit, even to himself, that Tamar might be right about something; they still could use a few more shekels flowing into his money bag right now. He couldn't be in two places at the same time, and so while he wanted to spend more time with Judas, his leather-work trade could not afford to suffer.

~~~

With his leg fully healed and by focusing on his work more, business got better, and so a few months later Barabbas decided he could take some time off to go back to listen to Jesus again. He had just finished eating, and he got up from the table. Then he went to the window and looked out at the ledge he so enjoyed climbing to.

Tamar watched him. "I like it when you're here more."

Barabbas quickly half turned his head toward her. "Didn't have much choice between my leg and needing to catch up in the leather shop."

"But it's good that the business is doing better now, right?"

Barabbas reached his right hand up and rubbed his neck. His neck was a little stiff, and he had heard and felt a crunching of his neck bones when he had turned toward his wife. "Yes; there's only one problem."

Tamar felt a catch in her throat as she asked, "And what's that?"

"Can't be in two places at once."

Tamar's stomach tightened as she stiffened. "So what do you mean by that?"

Barabbas looked back out the window for another moment before turning again to Tamar, more carefully this time. "The business, no make that all businesses in Israel, will never be as good as they could be as long as we're paying taxes to Caesar and putting up with the Romans in our land."

Tamar inhaled and quickly blew a deep breath. "Not that again!"
~~~

Barabbas slightly leaned forward and threw his right hand upward. "What do you know about it? You think if we just hide our heads in the sand like ostriches that the Roman problem isn't there!"

"You may be right," Tamar agreed, "I don't know about that. But what I do know is the money situation is better when you are home working!"

"Due to my leg slowing me down," Barabbas countered, shaking his head, "and then the process of getting caught up in the shop, I feel like I've wasted the past year."

"Well," Tamar said sarcastically, "you may not have noticed, but our children are getting older; it costs more to provide for them now. You're right, it has been over a year since your accident, and I can say I think it actually turned out for the best. It took months, but you have been here every day and finally have the business going well again, kind of like it was after we were first married."

"And that's what it's all about," Barabbas' voice spilled bitterness. "Barabbas, the money-maker!"

"Try, more like Barabbas the provider, who took certain vows …"

"And I'm keeping them!"

"It was beginning to look like you were, until …"

"Until what? Until I start thinking about the future for our children, and grandchildren?"

"I  thought working in the shop was good for their future."

"And a future without the Romans will be even better!"

"Some people there is just no sense talking to!" Tamar was growing angry too. She could not understand why Barabbas felt the need to get involved in things beyond their town. He had a good business; he was respected, and he had a family to take care of.

"And like I've said before, at least a trip to Jerusalem will get me away from the dripping sound of your quarrelsome voice!"

"So you're off to Jerusalem?"

"Yes, Tamar," Barabbas said disparagingly, "I'm going to make a trip to Jerusalem."

Tamar stepped toward Barabbas and said more coolly than she felt, "Barabbas, how can I get this through to you? Business has been going well in the shop. I don't want you to start neglecting it again."

"I don't recall saying I wanted your opinion about my trip; I believe I said I am going."

Tamar's anger started to rise again. "There are still some things we need to purchase for the house, and when you're working every day it makes it a lot easier to save for them!"

"That's really all you want me to work for, isn't it?" Barabbas sneered.  "So you can make your trips to the marketplace and spend it all!"

"And again, I believe some people would call it trying to provide a nice home for our family."

Barabbas snorted. "If you had provided me with more sons, and would quarrel less, that would be nice enough for me! And, oh," he added, "it would also be nice if you had some fish and bread ready for me when I get home."

"And when will that be?"

"Doesn't matter," Barabbas retorted. "Just have something ready for me to eat!" He slammed the door as he stomped out.

~ ~ ~

Tamar sank into a chair and leaned against the table, her cheekbones resting against her open palms. After a couple of moments she got up from the table and started to straighten up a few things, talking out loud to herself, sarcastically mocking Barabbas. "I am thinking about our children's future, Tamar." She paused, and then replied to herself. "No you're not! You'd rather run off to Jerusalem so you don't have to work! It's more fun – for you that is – to spend your time talking with your friends about revolutions, insur-rections!" Tamar was so preoccupied with her thoughts she did not hear a knock on the door. "Just never grew up, that's what it is! Still think you're little boys pretending to be King David, or Gideon!"

"Anyone home? Keren asked as she peered around the edge of the door.

Not hearing her neighbor, Tamar continued her tirade. "And by the way, Tamar, it would be nice if you had some fish and bread ready when I get home." "Of course, Barabbas, and, if you don't mind, please, when will that be?" "Doesn't matter, Tamar, just have something ready."

"Fighting again?"

Tamar jumped and clutched her chest. "Oh, Keren, you startled me; I didn't see you."

"Or hear me. I knocked, and then asked if anyone was here."

"How long were you there?"

Keren laughed, "Oh, I guess since about King David, or Gideon."

"I'd ask you to come on in, but I guess you already are. Instead, have a seat." Keren laughed and sat at the table opposite Tamar. "Barabbas just makes me so angry sometimes!"

"I thought just yesterday you said things seemed to be getting better."

"I guess," Tamar snorted, "the important part of the phrase was 'seemed to be getting better', but, today, no, obviously not so."

Keren shook her head affirmatively. "Fighting again," she said.

"Well, what would you do?" Tamar defensively asked. "The business is finally getting better, and so now he thinks it's time to run off again and chase dreams of a revolution. A revolution is not going to help the business. I just … Who's that?" she asked looking toward the door where a knocking was heard. "Priscilla, maybe?" Tamar got up and went to the door. "Oh, hi, Priscilla, come on in."

"They're fighting again." Keren looked down quickly when Tamar flashed a look of displeasure her way.

"I'm sorry to hear that." Priscilla and Tamar sat at the table with Keren, "I thought yesterday you said things seemed to be getting better."

Keren spoke up again, being more careful with her words this time. "Key word – seemed – actually, not so."

Tamar started to explain to Priscilla why she was upset. "A revolution is not going to help the business. At least not his. Maybe if he made spears."

"What about the leather garments and belts he makes?" Keren inserted. "Revolutionaries have to wear clothes."

Tamar leaned back against the chair and folded her arms. Her lower lip curled into her mouth as she thought about what Keren had just said. "That might actually work, if he'd stay here and make them. But, no, he wants to be a leader, do something important, and make his life meaningful!"

" I guess," Priscilla said, "feeling like life is meaningful seems to be something everyone wants."

"Well," Tamar continued, "he could try to be a leader, in this house – a leader, not a king, a leader." She leaned forward and rested her elbows on the table. "And if he wants something meaningful to do, something to feel important about, maybe he could spend more time with his children."

"I guess," Priscilla said, "Hizkiah would agree with you on that, especially the last part."

"So why can't Barabbas?" Tamar's voice started to sound venomous. "But, no, off to Jerusalem, chasing revolutions and insurrections."

~~~

On the five-mile trip to Jerusalem, Barabbas thought a lot about his seemingly constant arguments with Tamar. All he wanted to do was be involved in action that would usher in the kingdom of God, and it seemed to him that all she wanted him to do was work harder to bring home money so she could go to the market and get things for herself and the children. There seemed to be no room for compromise; it was either stay at home more with his wife and children, or work to bring in a new kingdom, one that would make things right and put the men back in charge of things again. He decided he'd rather spend his time bringing in the kingdom of God. As he approached the crowd that had gathered to hear Jesus, Judas spotted him and laughingly called out, "Well, look who's back. Couldn't stay away, could you?"

"I don't know," Barabbas shrugged sheepishly. "There's something about Jesus that keeps bringing me back to him. I think it's his boldness. The average person likes the way he cuts down the religious leaders. He puts into words what we all think sometimes. But, Judas," Barabbas shook his head, "I still wonder if he's staging a revolution against Rome, or the Jewish leaders."

"Well, Barabbas," Judas started, "you can't put new wine into old wine-skins else the wine-skins will burst and spill the wine."

Barabbas threw his hands up in exasperation. "What's that supposed to mean, Judas? You're starting to repeat his riddles instead of giving me a straight answer."

"Barabbas, you wouldn't know a straight answer if you saw one. Obviously a new kingdom can't be established with the old order in place; that there has to be new and different leadership!"

Barabbas rested his fist over the top of the walking stick in his right hand and looked down at it for a moment. "You make a good point, that, in all honesty, I hadn't thought about. Our current religious leaders are incapable of accepting anything radical. So, tell me, Judas, do you think Jesus is really the Messiah?"
~~~

Then Judas related a story so ridiculous, Barabbas was too embarrassed to tell anyone else for some time. "Listen, Barabbas," he began, "a few nights ago Jesus and all of us Twelve were out on a boat when one of those infamous Sea of Galilee storms suddenly came up. It got so bad, I'm telling you, we were all afraid we were going to die, except Jesus, who was sleeping. Then Andrew awakened Jesus and told him how afraid we all were, and Jesus got up, asked why we had so little faith, and then Jesus said, get this, 'Calm down.' Now he was talking to the wind and the waves when he said that, and, anyway, Barabbas, as sure as I am here talking to you, when Jesus spoke, the wind stopped and the sea was the calmest I have ever seen it!"

**A smile of remembrance came over Barabbas' face as he recalled thinking at the time, *Thank goodness this is Judas' story and not mine.***

Then Judas asked, "Barabbas, what kind of man is this that even the wind and the waves obey him?"

Barabbas rolled his eyes. "Judas, do you recall just mentioning wine and wine-skins a minute ago? Perhaps you and the others consumed just a little bit too much of it on the boat?"

"I understand your skepticism, Barabbas. I wouldn't be able to believe it myself if I hadn't been there! But I was, and I believe Jesus somehow has more power available than Rome will ever be able to muster!"

Barabbas threw up his hands. "Then why does he waste all his time with the sick, and the women, and the children?" He raised his voice. "Jesus, why don't you get busy with some meaningful work; get on with the revolution? If you do that I'll follow you anywhere, do whatever you command me to do!"

"Oh, hello, Barabbas", Jesus replied. "And in answer to your statement, you need to follow the father's commandments first."

"Okay, the code again." Barabbas shook his head. "I'll bite. So, tell me, Jesus, which is the greatest of the father's commandments?"

Jesus smiled and pointed upward. "Love the Lord your God with all your heart, and with all your soul, and with all your mind. This is the first of the commandments and the greatest of them."

"Well, I know that."

"And the second is just like it. Love your neighbor as yourself. Everything in the law and everything the prophets ever said hinge on these two commandments."

"Well, Jesus, I can love God, but obviously you're not familiar with one of my neighbors."

Jesus took a step toward Barabbas as he quietly responded, "I am very aware of the situation, Barabbas. One night you let the sun set in anger toward your neighbor, and it has since grown into bitterness, a poison slowly spreading through your spirit."

Barabbas felt a mixture of astonishment and anger as he asked, "How did you know about my fight with Jacob Bar Balandan?" He swung sideways. "Judas!" he demanded to know, "Have you been talking about me?"

"I swear by the stone David threw at Goliath, I never said one word about your argument to Jesus, or anyone else for that matter!"

"He didn't," Jesus confirmed. "My father revealed it to me."

Barabbas was angry with himself over the wasted miles he had just walked on another fruitless trip. "Well, Jesus," he retorted, "it appears to me that you, and this father you keep referring to, are prying into matters that shouldn't concern you. I think I can find better things to do with my time than wasting it listening to you!" Barabbas paused. There were others making plans for serious resistance against Rome, and he didn't want to bring unwanted attention to any of them, especially the man he had just heard about the day before, Eliud Bar Amon. He carefully continued. "I have heard there are those who are a lot more committed to bringing about the new kingdom than you, Jesus."

Barabbas turned to leave, and as he walked away he heard Jesus call after him, "I'll see you later, Barabbas. I hope you will find peace!"

Barabbas whirled back toward Jesus and hollered, "Peace, ha! How can one find peace when only confusion abounds! Your talk of peace is ridiculous!"

~~~

Barabbas was putting on his cloak. "Joshua, I'm going to the butcher shop. Do you want to go with me?"

"May I go, too, Father?" Deborah asked.

"Me too?" Tirzah eagerly added.

"No. You girls stay here with your mother."

"Why can't we go? Joshua is." Deborah's face was crestfallen.

"Because," Barabbas said a little too sharply, "he's my son. Perhaps I should say this so you understand; he's a son."

Deborah took Tirzah's hand and looked away so her father wouldn't see the tear starting down her cheek. "Let's go help Mother," she said.

~~~

A few months later Judas stopped by Barabbas' house for a short visit. He mentioned he was also starting to have some doubts about Jesus; it seemed like Jesus was, in fact, spending too much time with women and children, and that priorities in the cash flow seemed to be wrong.

"So, are you getting disillusioned?"

"I'm getting ready for some revolutionary action," Judas replied, "and I'm not sure it's going to happen with the Twelve."

"Are you sure?"

"I think I just said I'm not sure," Judas laughed. Then he got serious again. "But I have been doing a lot of thinking. Remember what you said about Jesus after John the Baptist was killed; that there may be some fight in him after all – it's just a matter of finding the right motivations?" Barabbas thoughtfully nodded his head. "Well, I've been thinking, what if Jesus was backed into a corner?" Barabbas looked somewhat puzzled as Judas continued. "What if something was initiated that forced him to either take action, or surrender?"

"What do you mean surrender? He's not even fighting."

Judas blew out a quick breath of frustration. "That's exactly what I'm talking about! Put him in a position where he has to fight, or quit giving hopes to those of us who are ready for revolutionary action. Let's face it; if they are false hopes then we are nothing more than dogs howling at the moon."

# CHAPTER FIVE
## The Exchange

One evening some time later, after the children were asleep, Tamar told Barabbas she wanted to talk to him about something Deborah had said.

"What's that?" Barabbas asked, as he rolled his eyes.

"Well," Tamar drew in her breath, and then continued, "Earlier today she asked why you liked to make her feel bad."

Barabbas stiffened, and clenched his teeth a little as he asked, "And just how do I do that?" Tamar knew an argument was coming, but she didn't care. She felt it was important to try and stand up for her girls. She loved Joshua, but she loved the girls equally well, and she knew Deborah was right in what she was feeling. "Like a few weeks ago," she started, "you asked Joshua if he wanted to go to the butcher shop with you, and when Deborah asked to go you told her she couldn't, and the only reason you gave her was because Joshua was your son. And then you went and changed that and said, 'maybe I should say, a son'. That makes her feel bad, like she's not as valuable to you as he is."

"Well," Barabbas retorted, "I actually think there is a place in our scriptures that says the value of a male is set at sixty shekels and the value of the female is thirty."

"Well, like I told her, men wrote the scriptures, and sometimes they interpret them the way they want to. If I remember correctly, the scriptures also tell how Deborah in the time of the Judges was a great leader, or have you forgotten something since you named our firstborn?" Tamar knew she was treading on dangerous ground but she didn't care at the moment.

"Let me ask you this, since you want to fill our daughters' heads with nonsense," Barabbas countered. "Did they list the daughters in the genealogies? No, only the sons."

"And where," Tamar shot back, "did those sons come from? Did the sons have babies? No, I believe only the daughters did."

"I am getting tired," Barabbas said, "of your quarrelsome ways, and, by the way, let me remind you that it says in the Proverbs it is better to live on a corner of a roof than to live with a quarrelsome woman."

"King Solomon also wrote," Tamar retorted angrily, "'How can one stay warm alone; but if two lie down together they will keep warm.' How can that happen when you are gone as much as you are, chasing after hopes of a revolution, always talking insurrection?"

Barabbas let a well of pent-up bitterness spill out. "Well, I'm sure you and the children will be better off without me, and I'm tired of listening to your nagging. I do know the longer you live with someone you can't live with, the harder it is to leave. Well, I'm leaving before it's too late. There will be an uprising, and I will be a part of it." Barabbas got up from the table and went to where he kept his cloak. He reached in for something and turned to Tamar. "Here," he said, "here's a bag of shekels. You stay here with the children.  I'm sure I can find work at a leather shop in Jerusalem, and I'll bring by more shekels occasionally to provide for them." Tamar stared at him in shock and disbelief as he put on his cloak and turned to leave.

As he walked out the door he heard the sound of a shekel bag hitting the wall, and Tamar crying out, "I don't want your shekels! I want you!" Her voice wracked with sobs as she continued. "All I want is a husband who cares for me and is a father to our children. Oh, God of Jacob, help me! Help me!" Barabbas set his face toward the growing darkness and strode out into the night.

**Barabbas leaned on his walking sticks and looked downward toward his home, deep in thought. He found out later his leaving had pushed Tamar to the edge of what she could bear, but at the time he had been oblivious to the pain he was inflicting upon her.**

~~~

The next morning Tamar heard a knock on the door. She wiped her eyes on the sleeve of her garment, and went to the door. She opened it to Keren and Priscilla. "May we come in?" Keren asked.

Priscilla quickly added, "Deborah came by and asked if I could come over. She said you were crying, and she didn't think you were okay, and something about her father leaving."

Tamar cast a quick look at Deborah, and then replied, "It's true. And, Deborah, it's okay you told them. But, for now, would you take your brother and sister outside, okay?" After the children were out the door, Tamar started crying again. "I don't know why I just couldn't have been quiet; maybe it's my fault!"

"What happened?" Keren asked.

Tamar gathered herself together and replied, "Last night I confronted Barabbas again about how he was making the girls feel. We argued again about his chasing ideas of revolutions instead of working, and he said he thought the children and I would be better off if he was gone."

Keren gasped. "Did he leave?"

"Yes. He said he'd find work in Jerusalem, and bring some shekels by occasionally. I want more than shekels; I want ..." Tamar again broke down crying, "I want a husband who will be a real husband – love me – and make me feel like I am loved. I want him to be a father who is as fair to our daughters as he is to our son. Is that asking too much?"

Priscilla chose her words carefully as she responded, "I don't think so. I have that with Hizkiah, and I know I'm fortunate."

"I guess with Salmon I'm somewhere in the middle," Keren added. "He's not as good as Hizkiah, but, on the other hand, he's not as bad as Barabbas – I'm sorry, Tamar – I didn't mean that to come out like it did."

Priscilla rolled her eyes and shook her head at Keren as Tamar sobbed even harder. Then Tamar gathered herself. "Priscilla, could
~~~

you watch the children for a while? I think I just need to spend some time alone, to get my thoughts together. I'll come by your place to get them in a little while."

"You know you can. Anytime. Come on, Keren, let's go."

~~~

**As Barabbas continued to gaze over the valley where his lifetime home sat, he recalled all the arguments he and Tamar had had before he left her, and the events that followed. Soon after he arrived in Jerusalem, he found work at a small leather shop, but, to him, more importantly, he was able to get up with Eliud Bar Amon. And he was correct; Amon was actively making plans for insurrection. Of course Barabbas joined the group.**

A few months later, after Jesus had been preaching again, Barabbas approached him. "Jesus," he started, "I'm here on behalf of Eliud Bar Amon to give you a chance to be part of some real action, not just teaching women and children. Things are moving to a head, you know, and we are going to have to pull together as an organized unit if we're going to win out over Rome. We are ready for freedom from bondage and oppression."

"The father is also concerned with freedom from bondage and oppression. Freedom for you, Barabbas, from your bondage to yourself, your bitterness, your pride, your …"

"Jesus!" Barabbas interrupted him, "I did not come here to be preached at! I came to make an offer, but since it's obvious you are afraid to be involved in some real action, we'll just have to do it without you and your so-called power. I'm sorry, Jesus, but I've searched myself, and I just can't seem to find faith for a Messiah anymore. I'm afraid any freedom we get will come only after hard work, sweat, and bloodshed!"

A tired look crossed Jesus' face. "You are correct, Barabbas, in fact, true freedom will only come after there is bloodshed."
~~~

Barabbas took in a deep breath and quickly released it. He got so frustrated. There were times when it seemed like Jesus was saying all the right things, but it didn't seem like his actions were consistent with his words. Words without actions were what led to Zachariah Ben Zadok, who had also claimed to be a Messiah, being beheaded by Roman soldiers. "Then why don't you join us Jesus? Doesn't it bother you that others may shed their blood ...?" Barabbas stiffened as he angrily interrupted himself, "Others, my eye! Jesus! I may shed my blood for your freedom! Doesn't that thought bother you at all?"

Jesus' look changed to one of compassion mingled with a sense of pain, almost as if he were somehow living out the words he said next. "Yes, Barabbas, it does bother me if blood is shed in vain. It would be a terrible thing for one to die and another to reject the fact it was done for him."

Barabbas thought maybe he was having a breakthrough moment as he earnestly pleaded, "Then join us, Jesus! This may be your last chance to get in on the revolution!"

"Barabbas, if I could, I would explain everything, but I can  tell you that very soon you will see things differently, and, fortunately, it is not your last chance to get in on the kingdom of heaven."

"Riddles!" Barabbas replied in exasperation. "Jesus, if you would just stop talking in riddles! Yet I still can't help liking you. Who knows, maybe we will work together someday; maybe you'll change."

Jesus smiled as Barabbas, turned to walk away and called after him, "Maybe, Barabbas, or maybe you will."

~~~

Jesus' mother was sitting outside her home talking with Mary Magdalene when Salome rushed up to them. "Mary! Have you heard the latest?"

"It depends." Mary smiled. "There are a lot of things happening. Which latest are you referring to?"

"Well, you know Jerusha; she told me her husband thinks there will be a revolution soon."
~~~

"Seems to me the more people talk about it," Mary Magdalene said, "the greater the chance of Rome finding out and squelching it."

"That wouldn't be the case if people didn't talk to the Romans."

"People talk." Mary Magdalene replied. "That's all it takes. You know how when the eucalyptus flower expands, the little cap formed by the petals falls off? Well, you don't put it back on the flower. That's the same way it is with words, especially those from loose lips. Trust me; I know what I'm talking about."

"Jesus has pointed out things along those lines many times," Mary added.

Mary Magdalene smiled amusingly. "And I think I know why. I believe he's had to deal with the same thing I did. People are quick to talk. Jesus makes no distinctions when it comes to who he eats or drinks with, nor does he judge people in self-righteousness, and so some people say he's a glutton and drunkard and friend of tax collectors and sinners. But they say those things without knowing who he really is."

Mary nodded in agreement. "True. Jesus says too many people make judgments based on mere appearances."

"So, are you saying I have loose lips?" Salome queried a bit peevishly.

Mary Magdalene carefully responded. She wanted to make a point without offending her friend. "I'm only saying it's easy to pass on information that may cause trouble for others."

Mary decided to move the topic back to her son. "I wish I understood everything going on. I only know these are dangerous times. I'm worried about Jesus."

Mary Magdalene agreed. "I'm also concerned about Jesus because there are those who think he is trying to lead a revolution."

"A revolution of the heart maybe," Mary replied.

"What is a revolution of the heart?" Salome asked. "Is it the same kind as I've heard Eliud Bar Amon is working on?"

Mary paused a moment before answering. "I, too, have heard that Eliud is trying to organize some men, but no, I think Jesus is more concerned with our thoughts and attitudes, and how we treat others."

"I believe Jesus will stay away from Bar Amon," Mary Magdalene said.

"Well, back to the latest news I was mentioning when I first came in. I heard Barabbas, the leather-worker from Bethlehem, tried to get Jesus to join Bar Amon's group."

Mary Magdalene asked Mary, "Barabbas; he was the one who got so upset when Jesus said he was not going to go to John the Baptist's burial, right?"

"Yes. Jesus has mentioned Barabbas. He likes him."

Salome blew a quick burst of air through pursed lips. "Well," she started, "I think Barabbas is a hothead and a troublemaker. My husband's cousin Keren, I know I've told you about her, lives in Bethlehem near where Barabbas used to. Remember I told you she said a few months ago he left Tamar, and his three children, mind you, so he could spend more time chasing these ideas of revolution and insurrection which seem to be all over the place. Well, she thinks Barabbas and Eliud Bar Amon are going to cause trouble."

Mary Magdalene nodded. "I know, Mary, you said Jesus likes Barabbas, but I still think he will stay away from Bar Amon."

"I think you're right; I hope so. I trust my son to make good choices, but I wish the times were different; I wish things weren't so dangerous."

~ ~ ~

**Barabbas stirred from his reverie again. Even now it was hard to comprehend how quickly things had started changing. Circumstances for him became revolutionized in a very short time period.**

About a month later, Eliud Bar Amon felt the time was right to make a move, and put Barabbas in charge of several other revolutionaries and assigned him the task of initiating action in Jerusalem. Barabbas and his followers were to ambush some Roman soldiers during a changing of their guard. Bar Amon believed a surprise insurrectionist strike swiftly followed by other seemingly random attacks would subdue the Roman contingency in Jerusalem before they could recover. Barabbas took the men under his command and made ready. As the Roman soldiers came down the narrow street where the ambushers lay in wait, one of Barabbas' men, chilled by the night air, sneezed, and the Romans were alerted. As the soldiers rushed their would-be ambushers, Barabbas thrust his sword deep into the belly of the lead man.

~~~

Tamar startled awake and sat bolt upright. She awakened from a dream of Barabbas slipping over the edge of his thinking-spot rock. She had tried to reach for him but he was out of sight. As she became aware of sitting up in her own bed she thought, *He's not even here, but I wonder what he's doing. Dear God of Jacob, what is my husband up to?*

~~~

The next day Barabbas was sitting in a prison in Jerusalem listening to a guard hollering at him, "Stirring up trouble is one thing; murder is another. Your King Herod is doing all he can to keep political peace in the city, and here some fool like you does something like this which may well bring the fires of Rome down on your own head."

"Herod!" Barabbas yelled back. "Ha! Herod and all the rest of the Jewish political hierarchy are nothing but puppets of you Roman dogs!"

The guard stiffened in response to the insult. "You had best be quiet!" he said as he opened the prison door and stepped toward Barabbas.

"Ha! You'll not shut me up unless you kill me, and even then my blood will cry out against your oppression! Dogs, I said; Roman dogs!" Barabbas didn't remember anything for some time after his outburst, since he lay unconscious on the floor of his cell.

~~~

**Barabbas decided to sit back down. After settling back against the Terebinth tree, he thought again of his arrest, and how the news eventually reached Bethlehem, and Tamar.**

She was cleaning house when there was a knock on the door. "Come in," Tamar called, and Priscilla and Keren entered. "Hi," Tamar said. "Good to see you. How are you?" Priscilla said that they were doing well, and then asked Tamar how she was.

"I guess as good as I can be. You know Barabbas dropped by a bag of shekels last week, but I haven't heard from him since. He was still adamant about insurrection."

"Perhaps he was too adamant," Keren said.

A look of panic crossed Tamar's face. "What do you mean?"

"Tamar," Priscilla said. "The children were playing outside and I told them I'd tell you it was okay for them to go play with my children."

Fear was evident in Tamar's voice as she replied, "What's wrong?"

Priscilla knew there was no way of gently breaking the news to her, so she just came out with it. "Tamar, Barabbas has been arrested in Jerusalem."

Tamar took a step toward a chair. "God of Jacob, help me." Then she paused a moment and put her right hand to her face with her index finger angled across her lips. She crossed her left arm in front of her and rested her right elbow on the closed fist. "I'm not too surprised, though; I've been afraid this would happen. So, what was he arrested for?" Keren moved toward Tamar as Priscilla responded.
~~~

"I'm afraid the worst. He killed a Roman guard."

Keren reached Tamar just as she collapsed to the chair and then cried out in shock, "God of Jacob, oh Barabbas, Barabbas." Her shock gave way almost immediately to anger as she continued, "Barabbas, Barabbas! Why? ... Why?" Keren and Priscilla stood one on either side of the chair and put their arms around Tamar's shoulders.

"I'm so sorry Tamar," Priscilla said. "We'll help you in any way we can. You know that."

Tamar looked up and flashed a small smile through her tears. "Thank you." Then she looked up toward the heavens. "God of Jacob," she cried out, "if there's any way you can help my husband, now would be a good time."

~~~

A few days later the talk of the prison was that Jesus had been arrested and was to stand trial. "Have the people revolted?" Barabbas asked a guard.

One of the guards laughed. "The people revolting? The people are a joke; they all deserted him; even his disciples ran off and left him. One of them, Judas Iscariot, was the one who betrayed your Jesus. Revolting? Ha!"

Barabbas was troubled, but at the same time recalled Judas expressing his frustrations earlier over the direction Jesus was leading the Twelve. So why hadn't Judas just left the group? It didn't make sense to betray Jesus, unless ... what Judas had said when talking about maybe forcing Jesus into action ... even under his present circumstances Barabbas felt a sense of rising excitement.

~~~

Mary Magdalene and Salome had just entered Mary's home. It was obvious Mary had been crying. "I'm so sorry," Mary Magdalene said. "We just heard about Jesus' arrest."

"Is it true Judas betrayed him?" Salome asked.

"Yes."

"Why?"

"I'm not sure, but I wonder if he thought he could force Jesus' hand."

Mary Magdalene looked puzzled. "What do you mean?"

Jesus' mother looked down a moment. "Jesus has so obviously displayed God's power; I think Judas may have thought he could initiate a revolution."

"How would that have occurred?" Salome wanted to know.

"By fighting back with divine strength when he was arrested," Mary replied.

"Well, why didn't Jesus fight back, if in fact he has God's full power available?"

"If he had wanted to, he could have," Mary said. "I truly believe that. But I also believe he knows God has a bigger plan going on."

Salome looked questioningly at Jesus' mother. "Are you implying that you think, at least for now, that things are 'all okay'?"

Mary Magdalene nodded her head. "I think I understand. Not all right as we see it, but all right on God's schedule."

"I don't understand."

"I didn't either," Mary Magdalene responded. "I thought my life was a mess. I was just going to eke out a miserable existence, and then die. But then I met Jesus and experienced his healing and forgiveness. You know, I might never have met him if things had been going well in my life. I think I was where I was supposed to be at that time in my life, and that is why I am here today. I don't understand everything, but that's okay."

"Nor I," Mary interjected, "but I do think you understand what I'm trying to say."

Salome snorted. "Well, I wonder if they would have arrested Jesus if that troublemaker Barabbas hadn't murdered the Roman guard. I think the priests arrested Jesus because they know he has a following and has talked of a kingdom, so they probably figure his arrest will send the message to the Romans they don't want any trouble."

"I think you're right," Jesus' mother said. Mary Magdalene added that it was all in God's hands from now on. "True," Mary replied, "but we mustn't forget, it always has been."

~~~

Later in the day Barabbas was sitting on the floor of his cell leaning back against the wall thinking about his father, who died when Barabbas was seventeen. As a boy Barabbas had worked with him in the leather shop, and it was during those times he was introduced to the writings of Jason of Cyrene. Barabbas' father would tell him stories about Judas Maccabeus and his brothers and how they fought against the Greeks and Roman invaders who tried to destroy the Jewish laws and culture.

**Barabbas looked down over Bethlehem at the house Joshua now lived in. Barabbas' son was thirty now, with children of his own, and he still worked with him in the leather shop. Barabbas had continued the tradition of telling stories of the Jewish struggles during the era of Judas Maccabeus. He had told Joshua how Judas fought against Gorgias at the forts of the Idumeans, and how in the attack against Jamnia, Judas and his men set fire to ships in the harbor that cast a glow seen some thirty miles away in Jerusalem.**

Barabbas thought of how just a few months ago he had regaled Joshua with the history of Antiochus Eupator, who came against Judea with large Greek forces of infantry, cavalry, elephants, and chariots, and how the Maccabees resisted, all the while using as a slogan, "God's Victory." Barabbas reflected on what his father had taught him, and what he was trying to instill in his own son, that Judas Maccabeus fully believed his help came from God, and he urged his followers to remember the Almighty was on their side. Barabbas
~~~

couldn't help a small smile of remembrance as he shifted position trying to get comfortable against the wall of his cell. Those times with his father, plus listening to the stories of the old men in the village, were what laid the foundation for his desire to be a revolutionary. He just wished he could have another day with his father right now to ask for a little advice.

A guard interrupted his thoughts. "Barabbas; does your name really mean 'son of a father'?"

"What's that you asked?" Barabbas jerked his head upwards.

The guard repeated, "Does your name really mean 'son of a father'?"

"For a Roman dog you do quite well."

"Trust me, if it were up to me I would be content to let you either rot in prison, or better yet, it would give me great satisfaction to see you hanging from a crucifixion tree."

"Well, then, I guess it's good that my fate's not up to you."

"But who knows," the guard continued, "maybe you are 'Son of the Father', who knows."

Barabbas looked puzzled. "What do you mean by that?"

"I have orders for your release."

Barabbas had been steeling his mind for punishment by death, so the guard's statement caught him by surprise. "Are you serious?"

Staring icily at Barabbas the guard replied, "I wish it weren't true; but, you know, your release does seem rather paradoxical."

"Why do you say that?"

"The reason for your release. It seems the main charge your Jewish priests could bring against your Jesus was he called your God his Father, called himself a son; 'Son of a Father', or 'Barabbas' if you will. So Pilate wants to release him as the annual Passover prisoner, as is your custom, but the priests and the people cry, 'Crucify him;

give us Barabbas'– you, son of a father. I swear you crazy people can't make up your minds what you want, but at least it saved your neck."

Barabbas was stunned. "So Jesus dies instead of me?"

"One 'son of a father' for another 'son of a father.' Sounds like a fair exchange to me," the guard laughed. "One Barabbas is as good as another."

"Except," Barabbas shook his head, "Jesus isn't a murderer. What he said to me about a month ago when we were talking about freedom, shedding blood, rejecting that – almost as if he knew."

"Move along," the guard told Barabbas. "You can finish your foolish babbling outside in the daylight, in the freedom of the sun."

# CHAPTER SIX
## He Didn't Hurt Nobody!

Later in the afternoon Barabbas stood on the outskirts of another crowd, outside the city, in the dump, in the unholy place, and again Jesus was the focus of attention, on the cross. But this time the people were shouting things like, "Kingdom … Behold the King of the Jews."

"You called God the Father … Come on down from the cross if you are the son of God!"

"He saved others … let him save himself."

"He trusts in God; Let God rescue him now if he wants him!"

Barabbas couldn't shift his eyes away as Jesus cried out in deep agony, "My God! Eli! Why have you forsaken me?"

Someone from the crowd called out, "He's calling for Elijah!"

"Let's see if Elijah comes to save him!" another voice added.

Jesus called out loudly in a voice reflecting the pain wracking his body, "My God, My God!" He then shuddered as his life left his body. After a while, some of the crowd dispersed. Barabbas just stayed away from those left and watched, his mind racing.

~~~

When Jesus died, Mary slumped forward as Mary Magdalene and Salome quickly reached out to hold her from either side. "Are you all right?" Mary Magdalene asked.

Mary responded through her tears. "He was right. Father, forgive them for they do not know what they have done."

Salome threw back her head and angrily asked, "How can you say that about the men who have just killed your son? And what about Barabbas? I just wish he were here to see all this. Maybe he'd realize all the trouble he's caused."
~~~

"No," Mary said. "Jesus said, 'Father forgive us our sins as we also forgive everyone who sins against us.' I'm starting to understand and see more fully what this is all about."

Mary Magdalene asked Mary, "What do you mean?"

"I was told so many things when he was a baby. An angel appeared to me and told me I would be overshadowed by the Holy Spirit, and the child would be called holy. John the Baptist's mother, my Aunt Elizabeth, said I would be called blessed by all generations, and then she called me the mother of her Lord."

Mary Magdalene's eyes widened. "That sounds a bit like what the magistrate Uzziah said to Judith in the story of how she defeated Holofernes, commander of the Assyrian army."

"What are you talking about?" Salome asked.

"Uzziah told her she was blessed beyond all women on earth in the sight of the Most High God." She turned to Jesus' mother again. "But Mary, forgive me for interrupting, please go on. What else happened?"

"Well, after Jesus was born, shepherds came to the manger in Bethlehem saying that angels had appeared to them saying a Savior had been born, and directed them to me and the baby. Then when we took Jesus to Jerusalem to present him to God, a man called Simeon, who was dedicated to God, met us. He said it had been revealed to him by the Holy Spirit that he would not die before he had seen the Lord's Messiah. He said he was moved by the Spirit to come to the temple at the same time we were there. Then he took the baby Jesus in his arms and praised God. He said, 'Lord, you can let me go now in peace because with my own eyes I have seen your salvation which you have prepared for all people. He will be a light for the people of Israel and Gentiles alike'."

"Mother of God!" Salome's eyes widened.

"You've never mentioned these incidents before," Mary Magdalene added.

Mary gave a little smile. "No. I treasured all these things and pondered them in my heart. Then, as Jesus grew, he and I discussed them. I taught him," she sadly smiled as a tear rolled down her cheek, "and he taught me." As she brushed the tear away she twisted her palm across her mouth and held it there for a moment.

"So what about this?" Salome asked, pointing to the cross. "Doesn't this negate everything you just said? And, furthermore, he never hurt anybody!"

Mary stared at her son hanging on the cross. "Jesus said that just like Jonah was in the belly of a fish for three days and nights, so the Son of Man will be three days and nights in the heart of the earth. We even said at the time he was talking out of his mind. I wasn't sure, or maybe didn't want to accept, what he meant, until … until …" She broke down in tears again. "Until this."

Mary Magdalene held Jesus' mother more tightly. "Mary, I'm so, so sorry."

~ ~ ~

Barabbas reflected on the events that had just transpired; everything he had seen, and heard. *I don't understand all that has happened*, he thought. *All of his riddles were just that, riddles. It looks like Jesus … was so horribly wrong … about everything.*

*Could this be? No, and yet …? The Psalm of David …"My God, my God. Why have you forsaken me? Why are you so far from saving me? All who see me, mock me; they hurl insults, shaking their heads; he trusts in the Lord, let the Lord rescue him. From my mother's womb you have been my God. Do not be far from me, for trouble is near and there is no one to help. They have pierced my hands and my feet." But, God, he never hurt anybody!*

~ ~ ~

Mary straightened up as she spoke again to her companions. "Simeon also said, in addition to the destiny of Jesus regarding the salvation of many, that a sword would pierce my own soul, too." She stretched out her hand toward her son and cried again. "And this is it."

~~~

Barabbas spoke softly to himself, "My God, my God, Why have you forsaken me?" He paused and then continued in his reflections. *His arrest had nothing to do with me, and yet the way things have become intertwined, I wonder if there was anything I could have done differently to have avoided this. But how? If it wasn't him up there, it would be me. It's supposed to be me; it should be me; I'm the murderer. He never harmed a soul. Yet there he hangs, outside the city, in the dump, in the unholy place, in what should be my place.*

Barabbas shuddered as he thought, what John the Baptist said, *"True repentance means being willing to admit that you are in the unholy place, that you are in the wrong."* He grimaced. *What Jesus said not too long ago, "It would be a terrible thing for one to die, and another to reject the fact it was done for him."*

~~~

Salome couldn't bear to look at Jesus on the cross any longer. As she diverted her attention away and looked around the crowd, she gasped, "Oh, no! Would you look at that? It's him!"

"Who are you talking about?" Mary Magdalene asked.

Salome practically spit out her response as she pointed. "Barabbas! I know I said I wished he were here to see this, but now that I actually see him here, I can't believe that he truly had the audacity to come and watch Jesus die. He's the one who is supposed to be up there. Mary, maybe you can forgive those who killed Jesus, but tell me, how do you really feel about Barabbas. He's the one who should be up there, not your son! I think I'm going to go tell him exactly what I think of him!"

"But," Mary interjected, "he's not responsible for Jesus being crucified; at least no more than any other human."

Salome threw up her hands as she asked, "What do you mean by that?"

Mary Magdalene spoke. "I think I know what she means, Salome."

"What?"

Mary Magdalene continued. "I don't know if you ever heard Jesus say this or not, but he said, 'Just as Moses lifted up the snake in the desert, so the Son of Man must be lifted up, so that everyone who believes in him may have eternal life. For God did not send his Son into the world to condemn the world, but to save the world through him'."

"Exactly," Mary reaffirmed. "That is exactly it. If anything, Barabbas is unique in that he's the only person Jesus died for twice."

Salome shook her head. "So that's all there is to it. It sounds good, but let's face it, there's a little conflict here between words and reality." She pointed toward the cross. "And forgive me for being so blunt, Mary, but the dead body of your son up there is the reality!"

Tears again flowed down Mary's face. "I know; in this world that is the reality. But I believe in the spiritual world there is another reality taking place that will supersede ours. I still don't understand all that is going on right now, but I have a deep-seated peace about all this, and I believe … I believe … that just like a corn of wheat is planted, and grows into something quite different than what was buried … I believe that soon we'll all see things differently than we do now."

"Salome," Mary Magdalene added, "what Mary is saying is similar to the times of the Maccabean struggles when a mother was arrested along with her seven sons. They were tortured and eventually all put to death for their faith. I remember hearing the Rabbi telling that as the fourth son was dying he said, 'It is better to die by men's hands and look for the hope God gives of being raised again by him'." Mary Magdalene paused, "So, Mary, I totally agree with you, but right now I also believe that we need to go home, to prepare for the Sabbath, and to rest."

~ ~ ~

Barabbas sank to his knees as he quietly spoke, "As if he knew; almost as if he knew. Oh, God, I don't understand this, I don't understand what all this means, but like the prophet Jeremiah I admit, 'I know, O Lord, that a man's life is not his own; it is not for a man to direct his steps. Correct me, Lord, but only with justice, not in your anger, lest you reduce me to nothing'."

"Are you all right?" Barabbas looked up to see who had spoken and was looking at a young boy who appeared to be about ten, and two girls, one about six, one maybe twelve, standing next to him. They were dressed in ragged clothes and looked like they were perhaps sibling orphan beggars. For a moment Barabbas wondered why his children were there, and then realized these children weren't his. Again the little boy, it was the sound of the same voice, asked, "Are you all right?"

Barabbas slowly rose to his feet and then replied, "Yes, I am; I am now."

"Did you see what they done to him?" the youngest girl asking in a quivering voice as she pointed toward the cross. She had tears rolling down her cheek. "Why did they do that? He was good to us; a couple times we were close enough to be held by him as he told us stories. He didn't hurt nobody! Once he told us a story about a lost sheep, and he even put me on his shoulders." She started sobbing. "He didn't hurt nobody; he didn't hurt nobody!"

The little boy's nostrils flared. "I heard the priests did this. They had a chance to free him, but instead freed that murderer, Barabbas. That's what I heard. Have you heard that, mister?"

Barabbas' cheeks flushed. "I think you're right, son; I heard that, too." He looked at the girl who had spoken, and added, "And you're right, too. He never hurt anybody."

"You don't have a coin so we could buy some bread, do you, mister?" the boy asked.

Barabbas sadly looked down. "No, I don't. I've not been working the past few days, and I'm all out of coins myself. But do you know where the street is that Eliud Bar Ammon lives on?"

"I don't like him. We asked him for coins once, and he chased us away; said he had more important things to do than bother with orphans."

Barabbas' face showed a hint of a smile. "Well, I'm not sending you to him. But two houses north of where he lives, in the direction of the temple, there is a house where an older couple live, Samuel Bar Zachriah and his wife Jerusha. I hear they are kind people, and they might be able to help you."

"Should we tell them who sent us?"

Barabbas thought of what the boy had unknowingly said about him a moment ago. He didn't have time to explain to children about things he wouldn't have even been able to explain to adults. "No, just tell them it was someone you saw at the Jesus crucifixion."

Barabbas watched as the children walked away. Tears started to flow down his cheeks as he was overwhelmed with homesickness for his children, his son and his two girls. "As soon as I find out a couple things, things I must clarify," again he quietly spoke, "I'm going back home; I want to see my family again."

**Barabbas stood again, and wondered as he had so many times before, about the three children who talked to him near the crucifixion site. He checked with his friends Samuel and Jerusha and they said the children never stopped by their house. Barabbas asked several other people in Jerusalem, and no one had seen the children, nor did they recall seeing three children fitting the description Barabbas gave them even before the crucifixion events. Barabbas thought they looked like the children Jesus had told the story of the lost sheep to one day, but he asked a couple of other men that he knew were in the crowd that day, and they said**

they didn't recall a time with just three children alone with Jesus. Barabbas sighed. *Just another one of the mysteries of my life that hopefully I can get clarified someday,* he thought. *Angels, maybe?* He shrugged and looked off toward Jerusalem again.

# CHAPTER SEVEN
# Revolution of the Heart

Later, the evening of the crucifixion, Barabbas sought out Nicodemus. Barabbas knew Nicodemus was a follower of Jesus, and had seen him with Joseph of Arimathea taking Jesus' body away from the cross for burial preparations, and so he poured out his soul, and his questions. When Barabbas questioned why Jesus had to die like he did, Nicodemus responded, "Jesus will live again; he said he was the Resurrection and the Life."

Life. The word jarred Barabbas back to the reality of his situation. He had taken a life, destroyed not only another person, but that person's family. "But I am a murderer!"

"Remember what the prophet Isaiah wrote, 'Forget the former things; do not dwell on the past'."

Barabbas shook his head. "That's easy to say, but the fact is, I took another man's life, and I deserve to die."

"But," Nicodemus reached out and put a hand on Barabbas' shoulder, "Jesus took your place. And the Prophets and the Law teach we all fall short of God's holiness, which is exactly why Jesus died – for us."

Barabbas' shoulders slumped as he looked down and slowly shook his head. "But, still, look what I've done." He was truly sincere in his questioning. He paused a moment. "Do you really think God will accept me?"

"Barabbas, you, especially, are a unique person. Think about this. You, of all people born into this world, so far, and yet to come, you, have had Jesus die for you twice." Barabbas' eyebrows furrowed as he tried to process the meaning of what Nicodemus was saying. "Jesus died for you literally when the crowd called for your Passover release, and his death was also for you – and me – and everyone in the world. And, I don't know if you ever heard Jesus say this or not, but he said 'Just as Moses lifted up the snake in the desert, so the Son of Man must be lifted up, that everyone who believes in him may have eternal life. For God did not send his Son into the world to condemn the world, but to save the world through him'."

"But why, of all the people in history, was I the one whose life intersected with Jesus at a critical moment?"

Nicodemus smiled as he responded. "Some things we may never know the answer to, of that I am convinced. And I heard Jesus say once, 'The wind blows wherever it pleases. You hear its sound, but you cannot tell where it comes from, or where it is going. So it is of everyone born of the Spirit.' Who knows, he might have been especially thinking of you when he said that."

"Maybe," Barabbas smiled slightly, and then turned serious again, and choked up. "But what about Judas? I can't believe he betrayed Jesus, but still, Nicodemus, Judas was my best friend; we grew up together, did everything together. What about him?"

"I don't know. Fortunately, there are some things that are in God's hands, and not our responsibility. I do believe, as a result of my conversations with Jesus, God is not willing for anyone to be separated from him, and part of the plan he and Jesus devised involves reconciliation of all things, whether things in heaven, or things on earth. How that can work out, I don't know."

"Reconciliation … but … of … all … can I really be reconciled with God?"

Nicodemus chuckled. "I do know one thing."

"What?"

Nicodemus broke into a broad grin. "You remind me of my first encounter with Jesus; I went to him at night, I was full of questions, and I left with hope."

"Hope …So, I really can be reconciled with God?"

"Barabbas, again from the prophet Isaiah, 'See, I am doing a new thing! Now it springs up; do you not perceive this?' "

"Nicodemus," Barabbas responded, "as I prayed near the cross earlier today, 'I know, O Lord, that a man's life is not his own.' And now I believe it, for my life has been given to me again, by … the Father … and Jesus. Yes, Nicodemus, I do perceive this new life springing up inside. And I must … I feel I must try to contact the family of the man I murdered … they're probably in Rome … I don't know if there's any way of finding out … and … I guess … maybe a letter to them … to tell them I was wrong … and ask their forgiveness. And it's almost as if I can hear Jesus saying, 'Don't be afraid, Barabbas, for I am with you'. But," Barabbas hesitated. "Nicodemus, you are a learned man and know more important people than I. Furthermore, I know how to work with leather, but you know how to write. Besides, I'm not real popular right now. Will you help me with this?"

Nicodemus nodded his head as he quietly responded, "Yes."

The next couple days Barabbas was flooded with several different emotions. Nicodemus was able to find out from connections who to write to, and was told a letter could be delivered, so he helped write an epistle in which Barabbas asked for forgiveness from the family of the man he had murdered. After that was accomplished, even though he didn't know the outcome, or whether he would ever hear anything back, Barabbas was filled with a sense of peace. Nicodemus reassured him, "Barabbas, you have done all that you can; the rest is now in God's hands."

**Barabbas shifted position, and even though it was only recollection, as he recalled what news Nicodemus had next relayed to him, tears still came to his eyes.**

"Barabbas," Nicodemus carefully started, "I know you were close to Judas, and I'm sorry I have to tell you this, but not too long ago he … he hanged himself."

Barabbas choked up. "No, no, oh, Judas, what have you done?"

He paused a moment and wiped his eyes on his sleeve. "I guess, Nicodemus … I guess after he betrayed Jesus, he just couldn't live with what he'd done." Barabbas was silent for a moment and then continued, "Now I know how Jesus must have felt after John the Baptist was killed. Like I said earlier, Judas and I grew up together … and I've … regardless of what he's done, Nicodemus… I've lost my best friend." Barabbas put the palm of his right hand over his face as he quietly sobbed.

<div style="text-align:center">~~~</div>

**Barabbas found out later that, of course, just as word of his arrest made its way back to Bethlehem, so did word of his release.**

Tamar was eating with the children at the table. When Tirzah asked for more, her mother said that was all they had for the time being. "We don't have as much money with father gone now, do we?" Deborah asked.

Tamar tried to hide the pain in her eyes, as she replied, "No, we don't."

"But we will!" Joshua excitedly said.

"What do you mean?" His mother was puzzled.

Joshua got up from the table and went into the other room. A moment later he returned holding a garment and smiling proudly. "Remember, I was in the leather shop with father, and he taught me how to make some things. I know we have been getting a little money from the belts I've been making, but, this morning … well, I … I have kind of felt like we were running out of shekels, so earlier today I went into the shop to see if I could remember what he showed me about making a protective leather vest, the kind that soldiers might wear. I made this by myself. We can sell these, too, and get even more shekels!" Tears filled Tamar's eyes. "What's wrong, Mother?" Joshua looked crestfallen. "Did I do something wrong?"

"Oh, no, Joshua," Tamar quickly said. "I'm just … I'm just so proud of you."

Joshua was asking his mother why she was crying then, when Keren burst through the door. "Tamar! Have you heard the news?"

"Apparently not."

"Barabbas has been released from prison!"

The faces of the children lit up as Tamar asked, "What? How?"

"Well, the priests also arrested Jesus, charging him with trying to establish a new kingdom, and, anyway, it seems the main charge the priests could bring against Jesus was he called God his Father, called himself a son, 'Son of a Father', actually, 'Barabbas', if you will. So Pilate wanted to release Jesus as the annual Passover prisoner, according to the custom, but the priests and the people cried, 'Crucify him; give us Barabbas!' So Jesus died instead of Barabbas, but at least it saved your husband's neck."

Tamar shook her head in disbelief. "Keren, are you sure?"

"Yes. You know I've told you about my cousin Mahli, lives in Jerusalem? I know I've mentioned him; well, anyway, his wife Salome ..."

"The one who is a friend of Jesus' mother?"

"Yes. She sent word to me, and asked if I would tell you."

Tamar grew thoughtful. "Obviously I'm glad to hear Barabbas won't die, but I also can't help feeling sad for Jesus, and his mother. I mean, from what we've heard, he wasn't a criminal."

"No, and Salome said they crucified him between two thieves."

Tamar's countenance suddenly changed to anger. "So why isn't Barabbas here telling me the news instead of you? Nothing against you, of course, but if he's been released, then why isn't he here? God of Jacob what's wrong with that man?"

~ ~ ~

**Barabbas wistfully smiled. Tamar had been right; he should have gone home right away to let her know of his release. But there were so many questions he had had, and if**

**Nicodemus was correct about Jesus living again, they were questions he had to have answered.**

The day after telling him about Judas, Nicodemus told Barabbas he had talked with Jesus earlier that morning. Even though Barabbas knew he could trust and believe Nicodemus, he had to find out for himself if Jesus was alive. He went out looking, and in the early evening encountered Jesus talking with Simon Peter, and Thomas. "Jesus?"

"Barabbas," Jesus replied.

As Jesus said his name, Barabbas knew it really was him. "Oh, Jesus," Barabbas was overjoyed. "Nicodemus was right, and yet I knew he was. Ever since I accepted what you did for me, somehow I came to understand what you meant by a kingdom of the heart, a change from inside. I really don't think I could be any freer if Pilate and all his guards were back in Rome! But, Jesus, I watched you die on the cross. How? Explain it to me."

~~~

Tamar was numbly going through the motions of cleaning house when she heard a knock at the door.

"Come in," she called out, which was followed by Keren and Priscilla entering. "Hi," Tamar listlessly said.

"How are you doing?" Priscilla asked.

"Any word from Barabbas yet?" Keren added.

Tamar gave a huge sigh and sat down at the table. "No," she replied. She rested her elbows on the table, raising her arms and intertwining her fingers. "I'm beginning to wonder if God of Jacob even hears me." She kept her arms up, but released her fingers from interlocking, and placed her right hand over the top of her left fist. She sighed again and looked up. "I'm not so sure if God of Jacob is even up there," she dejectedly went on.

"Don't give up, Tamar," Priscilla excitedly said. "Listen to this."
~~~

Keren could no longer contain herself as she interrupted, "They say he's alive again!"

"Who?"

"Jesus! Can you believe it?" Priscilla asked.

Tamar shook her head in disbelief. "What? What are you talking about? Didn't you tell me he was crucified?"

Keren spoke again. "Salome says they talked to Jesus again, that he was resurrected!"

Tamar again shook her head. "I'm sorry, but I find that kind of hard to believe."

"I also am leaning toward the skeptical side, "Priscilla said, "but there have been so many people talking about all the miracles that Jesus has done, so maybe this, too, is possible. I don't know."

"But," Tamar scrunched her face, "for God of Jacob to bring Jesus back to life? You know, maybe I could believe this story if I had seen him perform another miracle, the one I need."

Keren wrinkled her brow. "What are you talking about, Tamar?"

Tamar gave a small sarcastic laugh. "What about the miracle of bringing my marriage back to life? Barabbas has been free for a few days now, and it is only a five-mile walk from Jerusalem to here. New life! Ha! People saw Jesus being crucified, and now some say he lives again. How? Explain it to me."

~ ~ ~

"Barabbas," Jesus said. "Let me compare myself to a kernel of grain being planted, and how it grows into a stalk, quite different from what was buried. In the same way I was buried and now live again, conquering death. And God has begun a new life and work in you, Barabbas that he will carry on to completion. Barabbas, the Father and I want to work on your attitude and treatment of others. The real kingdom is going to change your life ... from the inside out."

Barabbas looked hard at Jesus. "For whatever reason, Jesus, my life has been very involved with yours, or yours with mine, whichever, but, anyway, now that your new kingdom is underway…" Barabbas paused, then decided to go ahead with the question, "Will I be doing something significant in it? I mean I know I can't be a part of the Twelve. I know I haven't had all the teaching they have had, but still, will I be doing something significant in the kingdom?"

Barabbas realized Jesus' answer came as no surprise to him. "Yes, Barabbas, you will. Maybe not in society's sense of greatness, but in the Father's sense. Remember paradoxes. Go back to your wife Tamar, and your children. Be a good husband, and a good father. This is now your first and foremost calling. Love your wife as you love yourself. Don't be harsh with Tamar, but gentle, and understanding. You are united with her and she is your partner. Treat your two daughters the same as your son. The Father sees them as equals; you should, too. Don't exasperate your children, and you will create in them a thirst for what is right. Don't be afraid to admit when you are wrong, and ask for forgiveness as necessary, from Tamar, or from the children. This will be learning true righteousness. When you are learning and growing, you will make mistakes; that's okay. Learn from them and go on. In repentance is your salvation, and in trust is your strength."

Jesus paused, and then added, "And something else, Barabbas. Take time for your children. You are already aware of how quickly they grow. One of these days, who knows, you may have to reach up to give them a hug."

"So what rules do I follow?"

"My rules are written in the heart, the rules of a new covenant. Read the writings of Solomon for guiding wisdom, and, also understand that the prophet Micah summarized all of my Father's rules when he wrote, 'To act justly and to love mercy and to walk humbly with your God'."

"When will I see you again?"

"Later. It will be several years, but I will see you later." Jesus reached out, put both hands on Barabbas' shoulders, and looked straight into his eyes before embracing him. As they parted, Jesus said, "I'm going back to the Father soon to make things ready. In the meantime, enjoy your family."

<p style="text-align:center">~~~</p>

**Even though it had happened years earlier, Barabbas still remembered the apprehension he felt as he approached his home. Would Tamar even want him anymore? After all, he was a murderer; just because he got out of prison didn't change that fact. She might be afraid of him; the children, they might be, too.**

The day after his conversation with Jesus, Barabbas slowly entered his house. "Tamar?"

Tamar swung around from the bread she was making with a slight look of fear. "Barabbas! I've been wondering about you ... where you were. I ... I heard about your ... ah ... trouble... in Jerusalem."

"Have you heard about Jesus?"

"Well, I have heard that Jesus, in effect, took your place when you were sentenced to die, and that you were pardoned, and just a little bit ago I heard, I know this sounds crazy, but I heard stories that Jesus is alive again, but I don't see how that can be."

Barabbas reached for his wife. "They're not stories, Tamar. It's true; he is alive! I've met with him, and he is Messiah, leader of a revolution of the heart, and changed attitudes! Tamar, I'm so sorry over the way I have treated you. I love you, and I'm looking forward to what we can become together."

Barabbas pulled Tamar closely to him and realized he couldn't describe how free and complete he felt inside, as Tamar clung to him and whispered, "Barabbas, Barabbas. Dear God of Jacob, thank you. Oh, Barabbas."

~ ~ ~

Barabbas stirred again from his reveries and smiled as he gazed over the valley below where he could see Tamar with two of their grandchildren, playing, in front of their life-long home. *And now, he thought, we've been together ever since; almost twenty years of learning, growing, loving, and we have raised three wonderful children together. And, I'm so glad they, also, are followers of the Messiah of the heart. I guess, he thoughtfully concluded, I guess Jesus did have some very significant work for me to do after all.*

He smiled again as he turned with his walking sticks. About five years after his fateful encounter with Jesus he had named his walking companions Faith, and Perseverance. He leaned on them as he walked past the Terebinth tree toward the rocks he had to climb back down in order to get home.

# About the Author

Basil Clark is a retired associate professor of Speech and Theatre at the University of Pikeville in Kentucky where he taught public speaking, theatre, oral interpretation, and interpersonal, political, and health communication courses. His interests lie in writing, gardening, hiking, art, and enjoying all activities with his wife Cora, and their eleven grandchildren.

He served fourteen months as an Infantryman with the 1st Air Cavalry Division in Vietnam where he received the Silver Star and two Bronze Stars (one for Valor.)

In 1983, he won grand prize in the Performing Arts Repertory Theatre (Now TheatreWorks, USA [NY]) for his play *Change of Exchanges*. In 2001, his story "The Town Drunk" was included in *The World's Best Shortest Stories* published by Quality Paperback Book Club [NY.] In 2007, 2008 he wrote a DVD script for use by 4th grade teachers, *Mars Invasion: Coal Camp to Space Camp*. The curriculum is approved by the KY Department of Education and coordinates with the Mars Invasion program at the Challenger Learning Center of Hazard, Kentucky.

## Other books by Basil B. Clark

***Poetic Healing: A Vietnam Veteran's Journey from a Communication Perspective.*** Co-author, Mark E. Huglen [Parlor Press, Anderson, SC]

Tells of the power of words to transform pain, loss, and even desperation into their counterparts. A poetic journey that will uplift and inspire. Clark's plays and poems are analyzed by Mark E. Huglen who offers insight, through critical commentary, into the five phases of poetic healing.

***War Wounded: Let the Healing Begin*** [Waldenhouse Publishers, Walden, TN] also available on most reading devices as an E-Book.

A compendium of interviews and poetry examining paths of recovery for those afflicted by traumatic experiences, be they scars of war, loss, addiction, illness, or other tragic events. Features over 100 examples of subjective inner-wounding battles with which people have dealt.

## Characters Come Alive

Basil also has developed and performs several character monologues ranging from twenty to forty minutes in length.

**Presidents:** Abraham Lincoln, U.S. Grant, James A. Garfield

**Biblical:** Adam, Moses, Jepthah, Naaman, Job, Jonah, Mordecai, Micah, King Solomon, Nebuchadnezzar, Joseph the Carpenter, Barabbas, Peter, and Paul

**Historical:** Dr. Thomas Walker (early Kentucky explorer)

**Other:** Cpt'n B (Pirate)

CLARK IN CHARACTER as, left, Dr. Thomas Walker with Cora Clark; right, President Abraham Lincoln

## Speaking Engagements

Basil B. Clark uniquely addresses the very subjective areas of inner woundings most of us seem to encounter in our daily walks of life. He challenges audiences to recognize that in our diversity of experiences we find just how much we have in common, and to embrace the fact that the difficult circumstances we find ourselves in may, in fact, be laying the groundwork to relate to and help someone else in the future – in other words, to make beauty from our scars.

GoudyOlSt BT on LSI 50#CrémeWhite
Type and Design by Karen Paul Stone

Printed in the USA
CPSIA information can be obtained
at www.ICGtesting.com
CBHW020005251124
17752CB00008B/14